SONGS AND BALLADS OF THE
MAINE LUMBERJACKS

LONDON : HUMPHREY MILFORD

OXFORD UNIVERSITY PRESS

Songs and Ballads

OF THE

Maine Lumberjacks

WITH

Other Songs from Maine

COLLECTED AND EDITED

BY

ROLAND PALMER GRAY

CAMBRIDGE

HARVARD UNIVERSITY PRESS

1925

PRINTED AT THE HARVARD UNIVERSITY PRESS
CAMBRIDGE, MASS., U.S.A.

TO

CORYDON

A lover of the Maine Woods

AND

PHYLLIS

who first saw the light in Maine

CONTENTS

Songs of the Lumberjacks

Old Ballads and Other Pieces

Historical Ballads and Songs

Contents

Maine Broadsides

INTRODUCTION

FOLK–SONGS and popular ballads are great human documents. They narrate, in unpremeditated art and verse, the experience of an individual or group, and are usually addressed and sung to this group. In "The Jam at Gerry's Rock," for instance, is related an event which actually happened during a lumber operation on the Penobscot River in Maine. The logs in the river had jammed, and "six brave shanty boys" and their foreman, young Monroe, volunteered to break the jam. This was perilous work, in which the men lost their lives. Only the mangled body of young Monroe was recovered. His lover, Clara Vernon, died of grief, and her last request, to be buried by young Monroe, was granted. The ballad opens with the direct appeal:

Come all you brave shanty boys, and list while I relate
Concerning a young shanty boy and his untimely fate.

The motif that gave birth to this ballad was love's tragedy. This is one of the most frequently occurring motifs. In this collection of ballads it is present in "Fair Charlotte," "The Jacket So Blue," "Far, Far at Sea," "In Blithe and Bonnie Fair Scotland," and "The Prentice Boy's Love for Mary." Other motifs in the lumberjacks' songs are the joy of their work, as in "The Logger's Boast"; and the tragedy of their work, as in "The West Branch Song." Then the heroic, as in "The Sandy Stream Song" and the war ballads; jealousy, as in "The Twa Sisters"; confession of sorrow for a life misspent,

as in "The Flying Cloud"; or banter, as in "John Fer-
guson's Crew"; and love without tragedy, as in "Mary
Aclon." Elemental emotions and simple interests, brave
deeds, adventure, work, joy, sorrow, love, life's romance,
life's tragedy — these are the burden of their songs. They
are typical and descriptive of the lumberjack, the seaman,
the warrior, and common folk. Thoroughly human, they
touch all hearts. Sir Philip Sidney, referring to the old
English and Scottish popular ballads, voices a widely
held sentiment, frequently applicable to these American
ballads, when he says: "Certainly I must confess my
own barbarousness. I never heard the old song of Percy
and Douglas that I found not my heart moved more than
with a trumpet."

The sheaf of songs and ballads comprising this volume
I gathered in Maine during a long residence there while
professor in the State University. Their resemblance to
the mediæval English and Scottish popular ballads
aroused my interest. At first thought, it seemed alto-
gether unlikely that conditions in Maine would be favorable to the growth of ballads of the old type. Such
favorable conditions, nevertheless, were found to have
existed for over half a century. Maine, be it recalled, cov-
ers a vast area: one of its counties, Aroostook, is as large
as the State of Massachusetts. There are large portions
of the state — wooded tracts, remote and somewhat iso-
lated from civilization — where, particularly in the lumber districts, the people are crude and primitive, and
withal, be it said, big-hearted and stalwart — an epic
age, as it were, neighboring modern life only, with hills,

vast woodland, rivers and lakes intervening. Way down east, for instance, there is a little flourishing town divided by the Machias River; on either side of the river is — or was a few years ago — a lumber camp; each camp had its crew or gang of men; each crew chose as its chief or leader one of its number who possessed most nearly the elemental virtues of the heroes of old, courage and physical strength. Whenever these crews came together, their chiefs would fight, whether there was anything to fight about or not. I have not found or heard of a ballad relating these exploits; but I am looking for it. The "Sandy Stream Song," with the preliminary description of its origin, given on pages 31–33, illustrates vividly the actual conditions which gave rise to that ballad.

The ballads from Maine in the present volume have been collected from various sources. Many of them have been taken down as woodsmen sang or recited them. They have been transmitted by word of mouth and have been traditional in Maine, some of them, for over half a century. As in the days of Homer, they have been handed down from memory within the family, in the lumber camps, and in the river towns, and have travelled with the singers of them, not only to various parts of Maine but to distant states. Their exact origin is often uncertain, frequently elusive of the most careful search, and at times frankly evident. "Bay Billy" was recovered from California some time before I had ascertained its authorship. "The Jam at Gerry's Rock" circulates among the cowboys of Texas, is known in several other states, and has crossed the sea to Scotland.

One bitter cold day in December, 1916, I went in search of ballads in the little town of Mattewamkeag. I had been told that men were there who had spent most of their lives in the woods or in boats in lumber operations. My arrival had to be previously arranged, for the lumberjack is diffident about singing his songs to one from the polite world. I was bundled up in a big fur coat and taken in a sleigh some miles into the country, to the home of a Mr. Shedd. When I arrived, he was out of doors in his shirtsleeves and without head-covering. He was over seventy years of age, tall, slim, and rugged, with gray hair and beard. Aware of my mission, he was kindly in manner and willingly consented to sing his songs to me. When we went into the house, he sat in a rocking chair with his head resting on the back, and, rocking gently as if to keep time to the melody, he sang, in a kind of chant, ballad after ballad, for over two hours. He sang as if he loved to do it, and he never hesitated, though all was from memory. Some of the songs had been taught him from the memory of his parents, some he had heard in the woods. So far as he knew, none had ever been printed. He had taught them to his daughter. I found it difficult to take down these songs while they were being sung. To facilitate my work Mr. Shedd good-naturedly consented to recite them. One ballad, called "Mary Aclon," was a favorite. The father and daughter sang it to me; then I took it down from the lips of the father. The quaintness and the simple charm of that singing abide with me but baffle description.

In another part of the town I found two other old men, over seventy, who had been woodsmen all their lives. One,

Mr. Fowler, boasted that he knew over one hundred songs, all of which he, with others, used to sing in the woods. Some of them were long, having thirty or more verses. It was interesting to hear him and Mr. Chadburne, the other woodsman, discuss the merits of certain rhymes in one of the ballads. Their facility as rhymesters surprised me. Mr. Chadburne remembered only a few scattering lines of the ballads. He explained that he did not sing, and therefore, "could not remember them." The favorite here seemed to be "Fair Charlotte," which Mr. Fowler sang in a lilting chant with unique effect. Miss Chadburne, a college graduate, took it down for me.

My most unique and valuable find was in a trolley car halted on a switch somewhere between Orono and Bangor. While we were waiting, the motorman came in and asked me if I would give him a copy of "The Jam at Gerry's Rock." I replied that I should be glad to do so, but should like to know why he was interested in that particular song. "Well," he said, "my brother was a member of the crew referred to in that song, and it is all true that is related about the accident." I was at once all excitement and curiosity. I pressed him — Mr. Reid by name, who had himself been a lumberjack — to tell me what he knew about the origin of the ballad. I wrote down what he said. "The accident," he told me, "took place on the west branch of the Penobscot River just above a place now called Mawutum. There was a rock there where the logs frequently jammed. The rock, I think, was afterwards blown up." The statement regarding the blowing up of the rock was later confirmed

by Mr. Perkins of Orono, who for many years had been
engaged in lumber operations. "Monroe and his love,"
Mr. Reid added, "are buried further up the river." Then
I asked him to tell me how this and similar ballads come
to be made. "Well," he said, "I will tell you. Something
happens. Then, at night, when the fellows are gathered
around the fire, some one, who can sing better than the
rest, starts a song, and the rest chip in. Each adds a
little, some make changes and additions, until the song
is made. Probably one hundred and fifty took part in
making that song. Something happens," he reiterated,
"then the boys get together, and some one who sings
better than the rest usually starts a song and the others
help." Mr. Reid made this statement without receiving
from me any hint whatever regarding the theories held
of the origin of the ballad. Five lumberjacks have confirmed his account of how the popular ballad came to be
made, and one added this interesting and significant fact,
namely, that an employer was in the habit of paying more
to a lumberjack who could sing than to the others.

For those interested in the theories regarding the origin
of popular ballads, and therefore in the value of the evidence here set forth, I may state with repeated emphasis
that, in seeking information from the lumberjacks and
from lumber operators, I in no case disclosed any theory
whatsoever or even asked, "Did you dance?" or "Did
more than one person compose these songs?" I asked
simply, "What did you do?" and "How did these songs
come to be made?"

On another occasion I put the same question as to how

the ballads came to be made to Mr. Perkins, previously referred to. He replied: "In general, some one person in the group or gang has ability superior to the others in singing or in story-telling. He started a song, the rest often aiding by adding a word here and there, sometimes a line or more. One Frenchman, I remember, would ask them [the lumberjacks] to give him an incident or accident or character; then he would rapidly improvise a story, I think, in prose. This man would hold the men's interest for a long period at a time, relating a story based on what was given him."

In seeking information concerning the mythical Paul Bunyan, the super-Herculean creation of the lumberjacks of Maine, I received from Mr. J. S. Baird of the United States Forest Service in Montana a copy of a ballad called "The Shanty Boy," which originated about 1847 near Muskegon, Michigan. Of the fifteen verses, I quote the first and the last. Here is the only instance known to me where a ballad relates the number of persons who took part in its composition. The authors are not known.

Come boys, if you will listen, I'll sing to you a song,
It's all about the pinery boys and how they get along;
A set of jovial fellows, so merry and so fine,
They spend a jovial winter in cutting down the pine.

　　*　　*　　*　　*　　*　　*　　*

So now my song is ended, you'll find those words are true,
But if you doubt one word of this, just ask Jim Lockwell's
　　crew.
'T was in Jim Lockwell's shanty this song was sung with glee,
And that's the end of "The Shanty Boy," and it was com-
　　posed by three.

The exact date of the composition of a popular ballad is seldom known. The date when a ballad was taken down should not be confused with the date of the ballad itself. The date of the "Sandy Stream Song" is established with sufficient accuracy as 1874; that of "The Jam at Gerry's Rock" can be approximated; that of the "Alphabet Song" is not known at all. In like manner, the authors are usually unknown. It is notable that the author of the "Sandy Stream Song" is only vaguely remembered as a member of the crew; his name and destiny are obscure. In all cases, whether the author is known or not, his personality concerns us very little, if at all. Even in "Peter Ambely," if Peter is held to be the author, the interest of the ballad is quite impersonal. Generally speaking, the author of a popular ballad is simply the medium, usually nameless, through whom a group gives utterance to its united emotion and thought, and to whom a group freely contributes portions — however slight and fragmentary — of the song. With this conception of authorship in mind, for the accuracy of which I have given the testimony of those who were directly or indirectly a party to the song-making, the popular ballad is to be thought of as a communal or group product, with one person, who could sing better than the others, mainly responsible for its composition. Specifically, "The Jam at Gerry's Rock," we know, through evidence, was composed by several. The "Sandy Stream Song" also, notwithstanding the fact that the author is vaguely remembered, was in all likelihood the product of more than one, because of the nature of the subject matter and the circumstances involved. "Guy Read," on the other hand, though the author is unknown, was probably the work of an individual and perhaps a woman — for here we have the indirect method of a letter, amounting to a literary device, and the suggestion of personal loss.

I have included in the collection some obviously modern selections: "The Dying Hobo," because it is too realistic a skit to be passed by; and several broadsides, because they illustrate a type of verse often thought non-existent in America. Mr. Friend, the author of several of the broadsides, I first met on a Penobscot River boat in Bangor harbor. He approached me with a thin pasteboard box under his arm. He sat beside me and, taking a sheet from his box, asked me to read it. This was "The Bangor Fire," describing an incident within my own experience. He was in the habit of selling these broadsides, he said, for ten cents. As he showed me the one to "President Wilson," on his second nomination for President, Mr. Friend remarked that he had sent a copy to President Wilson, who had, in return, honored him with a letter of appreciation. He also related how he had taken "Bar Harbor by the Sea" to the late J. Pierpont Morgan at Bar Harbor, and how Mr. Morgan, emptying his pockets, gave him all the money he happened to have with him. He told me the story of his life. He had been educated for the priesthood; but, finding that his physical and mental peace required a wife, he married, and he supported his family by writing verses on current events. These he printed with illustrations and sold them itinerantly. Here was a man over sixty, I judged, well dressed, intelligent, a kin of the wandering minstrel of old — or were the old bards always bachelors?

The man was unique in my experience. As he rose to go ashore, I was tempted to break my speaking engagement down the river and follow Friend up in Bangor. I compromised by inviting myself to his house upon my return. His home I found modest, comfortable, and attractive. We sat round the dining-room table, on which he had placed his treasure-hoard of verse. One after another, until we had gone through the little pile, he read to me with a good deal of spirit and pride, pointing out the merits of special verses or lines. As he read "Mount Hope Chapel," the tears streamed down his face; now and then he shot up his right arm and cried, "Ain't that grand? Ain't that grand?" However crude his verse, here was a man who felt in the depths what he had tried to express with the best art at his command. I bought his broadsides, some for myself and duplicates for the Harvard library, as Professor Kittredge had expressed a wish for them. I print them with the author's permission.

This collection of popular ballads is not to be thought of as complete or final. There are, without doubt, many more ballads still sung in the lumber camps or lingering in the memories of the aged woodsmen and seamen. Soon it will be too late to gather them; those who know them are rapidly passing on. Even now the type of lumberjack of fifty years ago is hard to find. We cannot expect an indefinite continuation of ballad-growth in Maine or elsewhere in America. It is, therefore, with a sense of obligation to American literature that I seek to preserve these ballads by bringing them together in this little volume, and adding thereto what I know about their origin and history. For some of the historical and bibliographical matter in the introductory notes to the several songs I am indebted to Professor Kittredge.

SONGS OF THE LUMBERJACKS

The Jam at Gerry's Rock

THIS ballad is widely known among lumberjacks. It had its origin in Maine (see Introduction, pp. xi–xii) but has travelled far from home. It is in Lomax, *Cowboy Songs*, as "Foreman Monroe," pp. 174 ff.; Shoemaker, *North Pennsylvania Minstrelsy*, pp. 72 ff.; *Focus*, IV, 428–429 (from Virginia). It has been found in West Virginia by J. H. Cox; in Michigan by B. L. Jones (*Folk-Lore in Michigan*, p. 4) and by Miss Alma Blount. It has also made its way to Scotland (see Grieg, *Folk-Song of the North-East*, No. CXXXII).

A

"JAM AT GERRY'S ROCK," *as taken down for the editor in 1915 by Mrs. F. H. Eckstorm, Brewer, Maine, who has several copies, all practically identical.*

1 Come all you brave shanty boys,
    And list while I relate
Concerning a young shanty boy
    And his untimely fate;

2 Concerning a young river man,
    So manly, true, and brave;
'T was on a jam at Gerry's Rock
    He met his watery grave.

3 'T was on a Sunday morning,
    As you will quickly hear,
Our logs were piled up mountain high,
    We could not keep them clear.

4   Our foreman said, "Come on, brave boys,
         With hearts devoid of fear;
     We'll break the jam on Gerry's Rock
         And for Agonstown we'll steer."

5   Now, some of them were willing,
         While others they were not,
     All for to work on Sunday
         They did not think they ought;

6   But six of our brave shanty boys
         Had volunteered to go
     And break the jam on Gerry's Rock
         With their foreman, young Monroe.

7   They had not rolled off many logs
         Till they heard his clear voice say,
     "I'd have you boys be on your guard,
         For the jam will soon give way."

8   These words he'd scarcely spoken
         When the jam did break and go,
     Taking with it six of those brave boys
         And their foreman, young Monroe.

9   Now when those other shanty boys
         This sad news came to hear,
     In search of their dead comrades
         To the river they did steer.

10   Six of their mangled bodies
         A-floating down did go,
     While crushed and bleeding near the banks
         Lay the foreman, young Monroe.

11   They took him from his watery grave,
       Brushed back his raven hair;
    There was a fair form among them
       Whose cries did rend the air;

12   There was a fair form among them,
       A girl from Saginaw town,
    Whose cries rose to the skies
       For her lover who'd gone down.

13   Fair Clara was a noble girl,
       The river-man's true friend;
    She and her widowed mother
       Lived at the river's bend;

14   And the wages of her own true love
       The boss to her did pay,
    But the shanty boys for her made up
       A generous sum next day.

15   They buried him quite decently;
       'T was on the first of May.
    Come all you brave young shanty boys
       And for your comrades pray.

16   Engraved upon the hemlock tree
       That by the grave does grow
    Is the aged date and the sad fate
       Of the foreman, young Monroe.

17   Fair Clara did not long survive,
       Her heart broke with her grief,
    And less than three months afterward
       Death came to her relief;

18   And when the time had come
     And she was called to go,
    Her last request was granted,
     To be laid by young Monroe.

19   Come all you brave young shanty boys,
     I'd have you call and see
    Two green graves by the river side
     Where grows a hemlock tree.

20   The shanty boys cut off the wood
     Where lay those lovers low —
    'T is the handsome Clara Vernon
     And her true love, Jack Monroe.

B

"GERRY'S ROCK," *taken down in 1915 by Miss Thelma Kellogg, University of Maine student, as sung by a lumberjack in her home town, Vanceboro, Maine.*

1   Come all of you bold shanty boys,
     Wherever you may be;
    I would have you pay attention
     And listen unto me,

2   While I tell you of some shanty boys,
     So noble and so brave,
    Who broke the jam on Gerry's rock
     And found a watery grave.

3   It being on Sunday morning,
      They did not think it right;
    Some of them more willingly,
      While others did hang back.

4   Six of those bold shanty boys,
      They volunteered to go,
    To break the jam on Gerry's rock,
      With their foreman, young Monroe.

5   When they got there to the jam,
      The foreman and his crew,
    The logs were rolled up mountains high,
      'T was a terror in their view.

6   "Prepare for action, my brave boys,
      Your hearts avoid all fear,
    We'll break the jam on Gerry's rock,
      And the rigging will go clear."

7   They had not rolled off many logs
      When the foreman he did say:
    "I'd have you to be on your guard,
      For the jam will soon give way."

8   He had not more than spoke these words
      When the logs did break and go;
    And it carried away these six brave boys
      And their foreman, young Monroe.

9   When their comrades at the camp
      The sad news came to hear,
    To search for their dead bodies
      In the river they did prepare.

10   And to their sad misfortune,
          Sorrow, grief, and woe,
      All torn and mangled on the shore
          Lay the head of young Monroe.

11   We picked it up most carefully,
          Smoothed back his raven hair,
      There was one fair girl among the rest
          Whose cries did rend the air.

12   There was one fair girl among the rest,
          A maid from Saginaw town;
      Her moans and cries would rend the skies,
          For her true love lay there drowned.

13   We buried him quite decently
          All on the tenth of May.
      Come all of you bold shanty boys
          And for your leader pray.

14   Engraved upon a hemlock tree
          That on the bank did grow
      Is the name and date of the drowning
          Of that hero, young Monroe.

15   Her mother was a widow,
          Lived down by the river side;
      Miss Clark, she was a noble girl,
          And his intended bride.

16   The wages of her own true love
          The boss to her did pay,
      And a liberal subscription she received
          From the shanty boys next day.

17   When she received the money,
      She thanked them every one;
    But it was not to be her lot
      For to enjoy life long.

18   Scarcely six weeks had passed away
      When she was called to go.
    Her last request was: "Let me rest
      By the side of young Monroe."

The Alphabet Song

THERE are probably many variations of this ballad. A is the complete form. B gives the same symbolic words as A except for 'S' and 'U'; B lacks the seventh stanza of A and the chorus. C, apparently from Michigan, is closely related to A.

A

"ALPHABET SONG," *printed in the* Maine Sportsman, *February, 1904, Vol. XI, No. 126. As to source the paper states: "Since the January issue, a reader who is too modest to allow his name used, but who has a lively interest in these old songs, has sent to this office the full 'Alphabet Song,' as he has heard it sung in the woods, and as it was written down for him by a woodsman friend of his."*

Regarding the chorus this note is appended: "The chorus was arranged to be sung, not between every two stanzas, but in the above version was given after the first, second and last verses, although when the lumbermen felt in the mood for prolonging the song, they would have to have the full chorus after every stanza, the entire crew bursting in at the first word like a cyclone; for these woods songs are productive of quantity, whatever a critic might say of the quality of the music."

1   A   is for axes, for we all know,
       B   is for boys, that can use them also,
       C   is for chopping, we now do begin,
       D   is for danger, we ofttimes stand in.

CHORUS
So it's merry, oh merry are we,
No mortal on earth is as happy as we;
Hi derry, don derry, hi derry dong,
Give a shantyman's grog and there's nothing
goes wrong.

2   E   is for echo that through the woods rang,
      F   is for foreman that leadeth our gang.
      G   is for grindstone that merely whirls 'round,
      H   is the handle so smooth and so round.

3   I   is for iron, that marketh our pine,
      J   is for jovial, we keep all the time,
      K   is for keen edge, our axes do keep,
      L   is for lice, boys, upon our shirts creep.

4   M   is for moss, that corketh our camps,
      N   is for needle, that mendeth our pants,
      O   is for owl, that hooteth by night,
      P   is for pineboards, we ofttimes lay straight.

5   Q   is for quarreling, we ne'er do allow,
      R   is for river that through our logs plow,
      S   is for big sleds, so stout and so strong,
      T   for the big team, that draws them along.

6   U   is for using, we put ourselves through,
      V   is for valley, we cut our way through,
      W   is for woods, we leave in the spring,
      &   so I have sung all I'm going to sing.

7   There are three more letters, I can't put in rhyme,
      And if it don't suit you, please tell me in time,
      For the trains they are moving, their whistles do
        blow,
      So farewell, my Darling, to the woods I must go.

B

"LUMBERMAN'S ALPHABET," *taken down for the editor in 1917 at Vanceboro, Maine, from the recitation of a lumberjack, by Miss Thelma Kellogg.*

1 A is the axe that laid the pine low,
  B is the boys that used it also,
  C is the chopping they all had to do,
  D is the danger that they are all in.

2 E is the echo that through the woods rang,
  F is the foreman at the head of the gang,
  G is the grindstone they all had to turn,
  H is the handle so smoothly worn.

3 I is the iron that marked their pine,
  J is the jovial that we were all in,
  K is the keen edge we keep on our axe,
  L is the lice that kept us from sleep.

4 M is the moss that chinked up our camps,
  N is the needle that mended our pants,
  O is the owl that hooted at night,
  P is the pine we always felled right.

5 Q is the quarrelling we never allowed,
  R is the river whose waters we drove,
  S is the sleighs so stout and so strong,
  T is the team that hauled them along.

6 U is the use we put ourselves to,
  V is the valley we cut our roads through,
  W is the woods we left in the spring;
  So now you have heard all I'm going for to sing.

C

"The Shanty Boy's Alphabet," *printed by Tolman,* Journal of American Folk-Lore, *XXXV, 413–414. Sung to Hoyt E. Cooper, Manilla, Iowa, by Frank Covell, who learned his songs in the neighborhood of Fremont, Mich. See also note to* "The Flying Cloud," *p. 116.*

1　A　is the axe that cutteth the pine;
　　B　is the jolly boys, never behind;
　　C　is the cutting we early begin;
　　And D is the danger we ofttimes are in.

Chorus
　　And it's merry, merry, so merry are we;
　　Not a mortal on earth is more happy than we.
　　Then it's a heigh derry derry, and a heigh
　　　　derry down.
　　The shanty boy is willing when nothing goes
　　　　wrong.

2　E　is the echo that makes the woods ring;
　　And F is the foreman, the head of our gang;
　　G　is the grindstone we grind our axe on;
　　And H is the handle so smoothily worn.

3　I　is the iron that marketh the pine;
　　And J is the jolly boys, never behind;
　　K　is the keen edges our axes we keep;
　　And L is the lice that keeps us from sleep.

4　M　is the moss we stick in our camps;
　　And N is the needle we sew up our pants;
　　O　is the owl that hoots in the night;
　　And P is the tall pine we always fall right.

5   Q is the quarrels we do not allow;
       And R is the river our logs they do plough;
       S is the sleighs so stout and so strong;
       T is the teams that haul them along.

6   U is the use we put our teams to;
       V is the valley we haul our logs through;
       W is the woods we leave in the spring.
       I've told you all I'm a-going to sing.

Drinking Song

PRINTED (without title) in John S. Springer's *Forest Life and Forest Trees*, New York, 1851 (Harpers), pp. 152–154, with the remark: "I present the following original rum song, illustrating the 'spirit of the times,' and of the log swamp muse." Shoemaker's text (*North Pennsylvania Minstrelsy*, pp. 90–91), as "sung by John Q. Dyce, Clinton County, 1900," differs in only two or three words.

1   'T is when we do go into the woods,
    Drink round, brave boys! drink round, brave boys!
   'T is when we do go into the woods,
    Jolly brave boys are we;
   'T is when we do go into the woods,
   We look for timber, and that which is good,
    Heigh ho! drink round, brave boys,
    And jolly brave boys are we.

2   Now when the choppers begin to chop,
    Drink round, brave boys! drink round, brave boys!
   When the choppers begin to chop,
    Jolly brave boys are we;
   And when the choppers begin to chop,
   They take the sound and leave the rot,
    Heigh ho! drink round, brave boys,
    And jolly brave boys are we.

3   And when the swampers begin to clear,
    Drink round, brave boys! drink round, brave boys!
   And when the swampers begin to clear,
    Jolly brave boys are we;

And when the swampers begin to clear,
They show the teamster where to steer,
  Heigh ho! drink round, brave boys,
  And jolly brave boys are we.

4   And when we get them on to the sled,
     Drink round, brave boys! drink round, brave boys!
   And when we get them on to the sled,
     Jolly brave boys are we;
   And when we get them on to the sled,
   "Haw! back, Bright!" it goes ahead,
     Heigh ho! drink round, brave boys,
     And jolly brave boys are we.

5   Then, when we get them on to the stream,
     Drink round, brave boys! drink round, brave boys!
   Then, when we get them on to the stream,
     Jolly brave boys are we;
   So, when we get them on to the stream,
   We'll knock out the fid and roll them in,
     Heigh ho! drink round, brave boys,
     And jolly brave boys are we.

6   And when we get them down to the boom,
     Drink round, brave boys! drink round, brave boys!
   And when we get them down to the boom,
     Jolly brave boys are we;
   And when we get them down to the boom,
   We'll call at the tavern for brandy and rum,
     Heigh ho! drink round, brave boys,
     And jolly brave boys are we.

7   So when we get them down to the mill,
    'T is drink round, brave boys! drink round, brave
      boys!
So when we get them down to the mill,
    Jolly brave boys are we;
And when we get them down to the mill,
We'll call for liquor and drink our fill,
    Heigh ho! drink round, brave boys,
    Jolly brave boys are we.

8   The *merchant* he takes us by the hand,
    Drink round, brave boys! drink round, brave boys!
The merchant he takes us by the hand,
    And *"jolly brave boys are we"*;
The merchant he takes us by the hand,
Saying, "Sirs, I have *goods* at your command";
    But heigh ho! drink round, brave boys,
    The *money* will foot up a "spree."

The Logger's Boast

PRINTED in Springer's *Forest Life and Forest Trees*, 1851, pp. 132–133, with the remark: "Loggers, unlike most classes of men, are under the necessity of manufacturing their own songs. . . . The following is inserted as a specimen of log-swamp literature, composed by one of the loggers." More or less modelled on "A Hunting we Will Go." Shoemaker's text (*North Pennsylvania Minstrelsy*, pp. 70–71), as "sung by Maine Lumbermen on West Branch of Susquehanna, 1850–1875," differs in only a very few words.

1 Come, all ye sons of freedom
        throughout the State of Maine,
    Come, all ye gallant lumbermen,
        and listen to my strain;
    On the banks of the Penobscot,
        where the rapid waters flow,
    O! we'll range the wild woods over,
        and a lumbering will go;
            And a lumbering we'll go,
                so a lumbering will go,
            O! we'll range the wild woods over
                while a lumbering we go.

2 When the white frost gilds the valleys,
        the cold congeals the flood;
    When many men have naught to do
        to earn their families bread;
    When the swollen streams are frozen,
        and the hills are clad with snow,
    O! we'll range the wild woods over,
        and a lumbering will go;

And a lumbering we'll go,
  so a lumbering will go,
O! we'll range the wild woods over
  while a lumbering we go.

3　When you pass through the dense city,
  and pity all you meet,
To hear their teeth chattering
  as they hurry down the street;
In the red frost-proof flannel
  we're incased from top to toe,
While we range the wild woods over,
  and a lumbering we go;
    And a lumbering we'll go,
      so a lumbering will go,
    O! we'll range the wild woods over
      while a lumbering we go.

4　You may boast of your gay parties,
  your pleasures, and your plays,
And pity us poor lumbermen
  while dashing in your sleighs;
We want no better pastime
  than to chase the buck and doe;
O! we'll range the wild woods over,
  and a lumbering we will go;
    And a lumbering we'll go,
      so a lumbering will go,
    O! we'll range the wild woods over
      while a lumbering we go.

5   The music of our burnished ax
     shall make the woods resound,
And many a lofty ancient Pine
     will tumble to the ground;
At night, ho! round our good camp-fire
     we will sing while the rude winds blow:
O! we'll range the wild woods over
     while a lumbering we go;
      And a lumbering we'll go,
       so a lumbering will go,
        O! we'll range the wild woods over
        while a lumbering we go.

6   When winter's snows are melted,
     and the ice-bound streams are free,
We'll run our logs to market,
     then haste our friends to see;
How kindly true hearts welcome us,
     our wives and children too,
We will spend with these the summer,
     and once more a lumbering go;
      And a lumbering we'll go,
       so a lumbering will go,
        We will spend with these the summer,
        and once more a lumbering go.

7   And when upon the long-hid soil
     the white Pines disappear,
We will cut the other forest trees,
     and sow whereon we clear;

Our grain shall wave o'er valleys rich,
  our herds bedot the hills,
When our feet no more are hurried on
  to tend the driving mills;
    Then no more a lumbering go,
      so no more a lumbering go,
    When our feet no more are hurried on
    to tend the driving mills.

8 When our youthful days are ended,
  we will cease from winter toils,
And each one through the summer warm
  will till the virgin soil;
We've enough to eat, to drink, to wear,
  content through life to go,
Then we'll tell our wild adventures o'er,
  and no more a lumbering go;
    And no more a lumbering go,
      so no more a lumbering go,
    O! we'll tell our wild adventures o'er,
    and no more a lumbering go.

The West Branch Song

TAKEN down by a student in the University of Maine, 1916, from the recitation of a lumberjack. Probably the west branch of the Penobscot River is referred to.

1   Come fellowmen and lend an ear
A melancholy tale to hear

2   About one poor mortal, he
Who has sunk and gone to eternity.

3   He hired out with William Brown
To help him drive his lumber down,

4   And up the West Branch quick did go,
Which proved this young man's overthrow.

5   He started out to break a jam
That had formed upon a rolling dam;

6   And as he started for the shore,
He fell, alas! to rise no more.

7   He fell into the dashing spray,
Where wild the waters do make their way;

8   And within three minutes all was done,
When the work of eternity begun.

9   Three times he rose, all in our view,
As if to bid us all adieu.

10   Our boats they being all on the rear,
We could not reach our comrade dear.

11   We put a boat in at the dam,
       We rowed three miles below the jam.

12   MacMann with the grapple all in his hand
       Raised this young man from his bed of sand.

Guy Read

TAKEN down for the editor in 1916 by A. B. H., at the time a student in the University of Maine. She was unable to determine whether the title is "George Read" or "Gee Read." From another source it appears that the correct name is "Guy Read."

1   Oh! well do I remember,
        One dark and stormy night
    The rain it fell in torrents,
        While the lightning flashed so bright.

2   The moon and stars above me
        Could not their light reveal;
    For dark clouds so gloomy
        Did their welcome light conceal.

3   The post brought me a letter
        I hastened to peruse;
    'T was written by a friend of mine,
        It bore me startling news.

4   For once I knew a fine young man
        As ever you did see;
    All in an instant he
        Was hurled into eternity.

5   He and his companions,
        Where waters loudly roar,
    Were breaking in the landings
        On the Androscoggin's shore.

6 They picked the face of one of them
  From bottom to the top;
 Full thirty feet this landing
  Had a perpendicular drop.

7 To work the face much longer
  It would seem a foolish part;
 A jar so slight, you see, it might
  This lofty landing start.

8 There were a few among them
  Who volunteered to go,
 To roll the logs from off the top
  To start the jam below.

9 This young man being among them
  With heart both true and brave,
 Not thinking ere the night would be
  All stricken for the grave;

10 Not thinking ere death's cold hands
  So soon should lay him low,
 To leave the ones he loved so dear
  In sorrow, grief, and woe.

11 The logs he quickly started;
  The jam it cracked below;
 It sped on downward to the verge,
  But would no farther go.

12 This young man now approaches
  The verge of the landing high,
 While all the crew with paled cheeks
  And trembling limbs stood by.

13   Up went a shout of warning,
         To warn him of his fate.
      He paused but an instant
         And seemed to hesitate.

14   He rolled the log about half way off
         When the landing broke like glass;
      As quick as thought he disappeared
         Into the rolling mass.

15   Quickly they rolled the logs
         From off his mangled form.
      The birds were singing sweetly
         And the sun shone bright and warm.

16   Strong men knelt down beside him there,
         Their grief could not command;
      Unbidden tears burned from their eyes
         And fell down in the sand.

17   Gently they bore him,
         Gently laid him on the ground
      Beneath a shady tree that grew
         Near by the pearling stream.

18   The bubbling sparkling waters
         Stealing o'er its sandy bed
      Seemed to murmur softly and sweetly
         A farewell to the dead.

19   The remains were buried
         By the orders of K. P.
      A funeral more attended, you would
         Scarcely ever see.

20   The ground and church were crowded
       With people, young and old,
    Once more to gaze on that face
       In death now pale and cold.

21   His casket was decorated
       With flowers, fresh and fair;
    His pillow, too, with every hue
       Of roses, bright and fair.

22   His brothers of the order,
       As they marched two by two,
    On his casket a sprig let fall,
       A token of the due.

23   The young man's name was Guy Read
       His age was twenty-three;
    On September the eighth was killed
       In a town known as Riley.

24   In a little town of Barian
       He is sleeping beneath the earth;
    He is sleeping with his kindred near
       The spot that gave him birth.

25   His mother died early
       When he was but a lad.
    They laid her down to slumber
       In a forest fair and wide.

26   Two brothers and a sister
       Possessing wealth in store.
    Sunny sky and music sweet
       Will not the dead restore.

27 His poor old aged father
  Now stricken down with grief,
 The joys of earthly pleasure,
  They would bring him no relief.

28 Untold gold and silver,
  Possessing wealth in store —
 Sunny sky and music sweet
  Will not the dead restore.

29 The robin and the sparrow,
  The sunshine and the rain,
 The cuckoo and the swallow
  In the spring will come again.

30 The blackbird and the throstle
  From a far land will soar;
 But one in death departed
  Will see again no more.

31 Now, kind friends and kindred
  Of him who's dead and gone
 To a better land in Heaven
  Far away beyond the sun.

32 His toils and trials now over,
  You scarce will see again
 Till you cross death's dark valley,
  The bright, celestial shore.

John Fergusson's Crew

As recited by a lumberjack and taken down for the editor by a
student of the University of Maine, 1916.

1   There once was a man
        In Howland did dwell;
    His name was John Fergusson;
        You all know him well.

2   He had a small crew
        Upon Meadow Brook.
    He was always a-rowing
        With the crew and the cook.

3   The first cook he drove
        Was Llewellyn Bean;
    The next was John Brown,
        Who would n't keep the camp clean.

4   Their supplies in the winter
        Was beans and codfish,
    And a roll of old butter
        That would n't stay in the dish.

5   The codfish and beans
        Took the place of fresh meat;
    And the butter was strong enough
        To walk on the street.

6   Put a piece on the table
        It would begin to walk round,
    And it took a cord of rock maple
        To hold the thing down.

7   The first to go out
        Was Milton and Jack;
     They made a big kick,
        And they never came back.

8   The crew that was there
        You could n't count in a song;
     And one roll of spiced beef
        Lasted all winter long.

9   Now we leave the old camp
        All covered with straw,
     Where the squirrels do chitter,
        And the hedgehogs do gnaw.

10   The lice in the bunks
        Do merrily crawl,
     And they 'll welcome the P. I.'s
        Who come back in the fall.

11   And now to conclude,
        And to finish my song,
     I 'll bid a farewell
        To poor little John.

12   If any jolly sportsmen
        Do come to explore,
     They 'll know Fergusson's camp
        By the pork rind on the door.

Sandy Stream Song.

As printed in *The Lewiston Journal*, Maine, July 21, 1917; from the memory of Edwin A. Reed of Orono, Maine, who is the "employer" referred to in the ballad. The *Journal* also gives a full account of the history of this song, and Mr. Reed's Sandy Stream lumber operation, an episode of which the ballad celebrates. I knew Mr. Reed and his family in Orono. Although the newspaper account is unsigned, I am confident that the facts have been authorized by the family, probably by Mr. Reed himself before his death in 1915, as he knew the song was in request. The following excerpts give, in addition to the history of the ballad, an idea of the lumberjack's life. "'Sandy Stream Song' was sung on the streams of eastern Maine for twenty years. For another twenty years it was forgotten. It was in safe keeping, however, for it was locked in the memory of the late Edwin A. Reed of Orono. He was the first operator of Sandy Stream; it was his crew that was burned out on the shores of Millinocket lake and he was the brave employer who led his crew to safety.

"The Sandy Stream operation was begun about 1874, if not in that year. At the time, Edwin A. Reed, 31 years old, was engaged with his father in the manufacture of shingles and lumber in Springfield, Maine. . . . Those were the days of crude, hard labor in lumbering. Sandy Stream had never been driven. For six miles at the upper end the stream was very rapid and it was a ten-mile stream into Millinocket lake. The telephone and dynamite were not then in use. With four oxen, some gunpowder and the old-fashioned fuse, the operators did what they could to clear the stream and build their dams. This lumbering operation took three years and was a financial loss in the end. The first year a crew of 75 men drove 17 days without getting out a log. Yet for a mile and a half along the wood road the logs stood 40 tier deep. The prospects of the season were shattered when the new dam above the falls (Hersey Dam) went out. This hung the drive and was a great setback. The dam had to be rebuilt the second year and this so delayed operations that it was necessary to return a third year to get the logs out. In the meantime the price of lumber went down so that the Reeds were heavy losers. They were many times advised to save themselves by going into bankruptcy, but the singer's hero was made of different metal:

> 'He fears no ills, he pays his bills,
> And things go merrily on.'

"The original crew consisted of 25 men. Later Mr. Reed came back to Springfield and hired 50 men additional. Of these 25 set out with Mr. Reed on the 20th day of April. The adventures of this crew are what inspired the singer. The crew put up at a tavern in Medway where they incurred the wrath of an ill-natured landlord by knocking some of the banisters from his rickety stair-rail. The landlord tried to collect damages but his only pay was in song. From Medway the crew followed the upper shore of the West Branch, across Millinocket Stream, then up to the tote-road to the old supply camp on the west shore of Millinocket lake."

"As the camp had been used during the winter, its timbers were fairly dry. The Reed crew made itself comfortable by means of a roaring fire in the fireplace. It was an old fashioned camp with a fireplace at the centre of the shack and a hole in the roof for a chimney. While the men slept, the fire soared and the camp caught fire. Everything burned. In the morning these 25 men and their captain were 15 miles from the driving camp, hungry, without food, and five feet of April snow. The snow was so deep and soft that the men were obliged to crawl on their hands and knees. For four miles they found it easier to wade in the river than to crawl on the snow. It was all hard work. The men took turns leading the way and breaking the path. All the crew became fagged before the end of the trail was reached, so that Mr. Reed covered the last three miles alone. He was the only one who knew the way and the only one who had the pluck to keep going. As soon as he reached the driving camps, he sent men back along the trail with food to meet those who were coming. The song gives local color to these events.

"The author of the song was a member of the crew, a cheap jack, but a good singer. His name and destiny are forgotten, except that he was finally guilty of some offence which sent him to Thomaston."

This map is also given in the *Journal*. From it may be traced the adventures of the crew.

1   Come all you river drivers,
       Wherever you may be,
    I pray you, pay attention now
       And listen unto me.

2   Of the hardships that we underwent
       We did but little dream,
    As with brave hearts we marched along
       To drive on Sandy Stream.

3 'T was the twentieth day of April
   We left the town of Lee;
Bein' full of fun and frolicsome,
   We jogged on merrily,

4 Until we arrived at Medway
   Late in the e-ve-nin'
To stop that night and enjoy ourselves,
   When all hands did begin!

5 The landlord then in one of his fits,
   Like a demon did appear,
(With eyeballs fierce and glaring,
   He would fill your heart with fear).

6 He ordered us to stop our noise
   Or quit his house straightway,
An' he'd keep no more an open door
   In that one-horse town, Medway.

7 So early the next morning
   Our employer, he did say:
"Come now, my boys, get ready,
   For we must haste away."

8 We marched along in single file,
   And good time we did make
Until we arrive at a logging camp
   At Millinocket Lake.

9 And some being tired and weary
   Lay down and went to sleep,
While others, being wide awake,
   Happened a watch to keep.

10 Simon Norton, being wide awake,
        When the fire, it first began:
    To put it out, he quickly said
        Was beyond the power of man.

11 The alarm of fire being given
        Each man sprang to his feet,
    With blinding eyes and wild alarm
        Took the first thing he could meet.

12 Some lost their boots, some lost their shoes,
        And some their hats likewise;
    Our provisions were our greatest loss,
        There burning before our eyes.

13 Our provisions being all destroyed,
        We waited for the morning gleam
    To pursue our way thru the rugged files
        To the camps on Sandy Stream.

14 When the morning light, it did appear
        Our employer led the van,
    And by his strenuous efforts proved
        To be no common man.

15 He plowed along most bravely,
        Though tired, weary and lame,
    Until he arrived at his logging camps
        On the banks of Sandy Stream.

16 Without loss of time he did dispatch
        A man with food straightway
    To meet these weary travelers
        And help them on their way.

17   Until into camp they all did come
         And forgot in pleasant dreams
      Their laborious voyage and loss by fire
         On the way to Sandy Stream.

18   Now we are safely landed
         And patiently do we wait
      For the blue etherial vaults of heaven
         To open their flood gate.

19   May the rain come down in torrents
         All with the morning gleam,
      And keep the foaming waters up
         While we drive on Sandy Stream.

20   Three cheers for our employer,
         All dangers he does scorn;
      He fears no ills, he pays his bills,
         And things go merrily on.

21   With this faint attempt at poetry
         I'll now conclude my song.

Canaday-I-O

A FRAGMENT of an old song given the editor by Mrs. Fannie H.
Eckstorm of Brewer, Maine, in 1914. It was given her by Mr.
J. Eldredge, Edinburgh (Howland) Maine, twenty years or more
prior to 1914. It was then regarded as an old song, and Mrs.
Eckstorm remembers having heard a verse or two of it in her
childhood. She places the date of the ballad at about 1855. On
the basis of these facts it could not be much later than 1859.
Shoemaker, *North Pennsylvania Minstrelsy*, pp. 76–78, gives a
somewhat fuller text, as sung in 1901.

This song is evidently the original of "The Buffalo Skinners" in Lomax's *Cowboy Songs*. Internal evidence places that
ballad at about 1873. There was very little, if any, killing of
buffalo for hides after 1876. In 1880 the buffalo were almost
extinct. Compare also a railroad man's song, known in the
eighties, printed by R. W. Gordon in *Adventure* for October 20,
1923, p. 191. The first two stanzas are as follows:

Come all ye jolly railroad men, a story I'll tell to you
Of the trials and the hardships of an honest railroad man
Who started out from Denver his fortune to make grow
Till he struck the Oregon Short Line 'way out in Idaho.

I was walking round through Denver one luckless April day;
Gilpatrick's man, Kercher, came up to me and did say
He wanted lots of railroad men and wanted them to go
To finish the Oregon Short Line 'way up in Idaho.

"Canaday-I-O" was composed, Professor Kittredge thinks,
under the influence of a well-known "Canada I O" which begins:

There was a gallant lady all in her tender youth,
She dearly lov'd a sailor, in truth she lov'd him much,
And for to go to sea with him the way she did not know,
She long'd to see that pretty place called Canada I O.

See *The Forget-Me-Not Songster*, New York (Nafis & Cornish), pp. 114–115; also *The New American Song Book and Letter Writer*, pp. 110 ff.; *The Singer's Journal*, II, 380. It is common in English broadsides (as H. Such, No. 164; J. O. Bebbington, Manchester, No. 324).

1   "O, say my jolly fellow,
          How would you like to go,
      And spend a pleasant winter,
          Up in Canaday-I-O?"

2   "A-goin' up to Canaday"
          Is what the young men say,
      "And a-goin' up to Canaday
          Depends upon the pay."

3   "O, yes, we'll pay good wages,
          We'll pay your passage out,
      Providin' you'll sign papers
          That you will stay the route.

4   "Or if you should get homesick,
          And say to home you'll go,
      We could not pay your passage
          Out of Canaday-I-O."

5   Then we had a pleasant journey
          The route we had to go,
      Till we landed at Three Rivers
          Up in Canaday-I-O.

          .   .   .   .   .

6   Then Norcross' and Davis' agents,
          They would come prowling round
      And say, "My jolly fellows,
          Why don't you all lay down?"

7   Our food the dogs would laugh at,
      Our beds was on the snow,
    And we suffered worse 'an pizen
      In Canaday-I-O.

THERE are eleven stanzas in "The Buffalo Skinners," of which I quote the first five as given in Lomax's *Cowboy Songs*, pp. 158–159, in order to show the correspondence with "Canaday-I-O."

1   Come all you jolly fellows
      and listen to my song,
    There are not many verses,
      it will not detain you long;
    It's concerning some young fellows
      who did agree to go
    And spend one summer pleasantly
      on the range of the buffalo.

2   It happened in Jacksboro
      in the spring of seventy-three,
    A man by the name of Crego
      came stepping up to me,
    Saying, "How do you do, young fellow,
      and how would you like to go
    And spend one summer pleasantly
      on the range of the buffalo?"

3   "It's me being out of employment,"
      this to Crego I did say,
    "This going out on the buffalo range
      depends upon the pay.

But if you will pay good wages
and transportation too,
I think, sir, I will go with you
to the range of the buffalo."

4   "Yes, I will pay good wages,
give transportation too,
Provided you will go with me
and stay the summer through;
But if you should grow homesick,
come back to Jacksboro,
I won't pay transportation
from the range of the buffalo."

5   It's now our outfit was complete —
seven able-bodied men,
With navy six and needle gun —
our troubles did begin;
Our way it was a pleasant one,
the route we had to go,
Until we crossed Pease River
on the range of the buffalo.

The Jolly Lumbermen

SUNG by Leary Miller, Lick Run, Clinton County.   Collected by
H. W. S[hoemaker], January, 1901 (Shoemaker, *North Pennsylvania Minstrelsy*, pp. 76–78).

1   Come, all you jolly lumbermen,
      And listen to my song;
    But do not get uneasy,
      For I won't detain you long.
    Concerning some jolly lumbermen
      Who once agre[e]d to go
    And spend a winter recently
      On Colley's Run, i-oh!

2   We landed in Lock Haven
      The year of seventy-three.
    A minister of the Gospel
      One evening said to me,
    Are you the party of lumbermen
      That once agreed to go
    And spend a winter pleasantly
      On Colley's Run, i-oh?

3   Oh, yes, we'll go to Colley's Run,
      To that we will agree,
    Provided you pay good wages,
      Our passage to and fro.
    Then we'll agree to accompany you
      On Colley's Run, i-oh!

4   Oh, yes, we'll pay good wages,
     Your passage to and fro,
  Provided you will sign papers
     To stay the winter through.
  But, mind you, if you get homesick,
     And back you swear you'll go,
  You'll have to pay your own passage down
     From Colley's Run, i-oh!

5   'T was by that tarnal agreement
     That we agreed to go,
  Full five and twenty in number.
     All able-bodied men.
  The road it was a pleasant one,
     By trail we had to go,
  Till we landed at McFarling's tavern,
     Full seventeen miles below.

6   But there our joys were ended,
     Our troubles, they began.
  Our captain and the foreman
     Came following up the Run.
  They led us in every direction,
     Through some places I did not know,
  Among the pines which grew so tall
     On Colley's Run, i-oh!

7   Our hearts were clad with iron,
     Our soles were shod with steel,
  But the usages of that winter
     Would scarcely make a shield.

For our grub the dogs would laugh at,
 And our beds were wet with snow;
God grant there is no worse hell on earth
 Than Colley's Run, i-oh!

8 But now the spring has come again,
 And the ice-bound streams are free.
We'll float our logs to Williamsport,
 Our friends will haste to see.
Our sweethearts, they will welcome us
 And bid others not to go
To that God-forsaken gehooley of a place,
 Of Colley's Run, i-oh!

Johnny Holmes

As sung and written by Jack McGinnis of Bangor, Maine, in John Ross's camps at Lobster Lake, Maine, 1902. Just how much help he had in the composition of the song is not known.

1   Come all you jolly lumbermen,
        Wherever you may be,
    I'll have you pay attention
        And listen unto me.

2   It's of a jolly barber
        Which I am going to tell,
    It's on Penobscot where
        This man is known right well.

3   He shaved three years for Hunter,
        A year for slippery Sam,
    He shaved a crew for Ross one year
        Down on Chesuncook Dam.

4   Then he went to Canaan
        To see what he could do;
    He got in co with Weeks,
        And there he shaved another crew.

5   He shaved six years for Loveland,
        For Smith a year or two,
    And now he's back to Lobster
        To shave John Roland's crew.

6   If he begins a-shaving there,
     The crew will let him know
   That they will surely kill him
     Or down river he must go.

7   When Loveland hired the barber,
     He gave him to understand
   He was to shave all the crew,
     Each and every man.

8   He shaved the crew, the bosses too,
     And all around the place;
   But the next he shaved was Loveland,
     And he done it before his face.

9   When Loveland found that he was getting beat,
     These words to him did say:
   "I think I've had you long enough,
     I'll settle with you to-day.

10   "I think I've had you long enough,
     Your pockets you did fill;
   They say you built two houses
     Down on the Baptists' hill."

11   He shaved the crew, the houses too,
     And all around the farm;
   They say he built two houses
     Where Loveland built a barn.

12   The year he shaved for Isaac Terrill
     When Gibbons was the boss
   He shaved the crew a leetle mite
     To pay for the mare they lost.

13 He shaved the crew a leetle mite.
    The boys they did complain;
    The one he shaved the worst of all
    They called him Bill McLain.

14 About the first of April,
    When Ross he did arrive,
    He said unto his barber;
    "Come let us take a drive.

15 "Bring your razor with you,
    And see what we can do;
    We will go up to Lobster Lake
    And shave John Roland's crew."

16 When he got up to Lobster,
    He met with a great surprise;
    It was there he met the little cook
    That blackened both his eyes.

17 Johnny stood and gazed on him
    With his squinted eyes,
    Saying, "Mickey, I'll be square with you,
    And that before I die."

18 About this jolly barber
    I'm going to unfold,
    He belongs on St. John river
    And his name is Johnny Holmes.

19 It's on the St. John river
    He begun his wild career;
    He robbed and stole, so I've been told
    And that's what drove him here.

20   About this jolly barber,
        He's of a medium size,
    His face is very narrow,
        A squint in both his eyes.

21   His face is very narrow,
        In his nose there is a crook;
    The Devil ain't a match for him
        For charging on a book.

22   These verses are not many,
        But I think they're very true.
    He never was in a concern,
        But he always shaved the crew.

23   He cut your hair and shaved you
        Without either shears or comb;
    The Devil ain't a match at all
        For squint-eyed Johnny Holmes.

24   If he shaves John Roland's crew,
        The truth to you I'll tell,
    He'll waken up some morning
        And find himself in hell,

25   With the Devil dancing round him saying,
        "Johnny, I've got you here;
    So you must go far down below
        And suffer most severe."

26   These verses are not many,
        But I think they are complete;
    When we get down to the city, boys,
        On it we'll have a treat.

27   We'll raise her and we'll roll her,
      With courage bold and brave,
    And with his poisoned razor
      Give us all a shave.

The Boys of the Island

A was sung in John Ross's camps, Lobster Lake, Maine, 1902, and taken down by Sidney Sykes, clerk of the camp. B is a fragment of a variant of A picked up by Mrs. Fannie H. Eckstorm in 1897 and given the editor in 1914.

A

1   You roving young heroes
        of Prince Edward's Island,
    Give ear to my ditty
        and I'll tell you the truth;
From a lumberman's calling
        it is my intention
To turn every honest
        and sensible youth.

2   The lumberman's life
        't is of short duration,
    It's mingled with sorrow,
        hard work and bad rum;
And if the hereafter is
        according to Scripture,
The worst of our days
        are yet to come.

3   The boys of the Island,
        on their farms not contented,
    They say, "Let us leave here,
        we're doing no good";

Their minds never easy,
    continually crazy
      To get over to Bangor
        to work in the woods.

4   A new suit of clothes
        to prepare for the journey,
      A new pair of boots made by
        Sherlock or Clapp,[1]
    A large kennebecker [2] all stuffed
      with good homespun
    And the brave Islander
      he will embark.

5   The boys of the Island
        in the woods are contented;
      The old bushmen gaze on them
        with a keen eye;
   "Just look at that homespun
      the lad is a-wearing!
    Is n't that enough to tell you
      that he's a P. I.?"

6   The boys of the Island
        are ofttimes in trouble,
      God, man, and the devil
        to them's all the same,

---

[1] May be bootmakers in Prince Edward Island or some other province of Canada. Not known in Maine apparently.

[2] A carpet-bag, such as the men from the Kennebec used to carry into the woods. Generally Maine men were contented with a meal-sack tied up with a string. To use a carpet-bag was regarded as "high-brow" and effeminate.

Such up-river tearing,
    blaspheming and swearing,
Drinking and fighting,
    't is their down-river game.

7   Brade Kelley will poison
        a man on bad whiskey,
    For pastime they will banish
        their lager and ale;
Then on the corner,
        when he does get frisky,
They will call for Tim Carey
        to take him to jail.

8   The mother of Moses and the law
        of this country,
    I've seen better laws
        'mongst the heathen Chinese;
On your little P. I.
        a man can get drunk
And then sober up
        under the shade of a tree.

9   It's true I'm a native
        of Prince Edward's Isle,
    I left my dear parents
        when eighteen years old;
It was my intention
        for all to do better
And to return unto them
        with great handfuls of gold.

10   'T is true, my brave boys,
  I 've made lots of money,
But the curse of all bushmen
  being on me,
Also my money it flew
  like the snow in June,
And back to the woods
  every fall I must go.

B

1   Oh, the boys of the Island
  they feel discontent,
The times there are hard
  and they can't make a cent;
So says Rory to Angus,
  "Here we 're doing no good:
"Let 's go over to Bangor
  and work in the woods."

2   Now the boys of the Island
  will work cheap you bet,
Fifteen dollars a month
  is the wages they get.
See their socks and their mittens,
  all knitted three-ply,
You can tell by their duds
  that they come from P. I.

The Lumberman's Life

A, WRITTEN down by a woodsman for W. H. Venning, Sussex, New Brunswick, 1904, was sent to Mrs. F. H. Eckstorm in 1904. She gave it to the editor in 1915. The ballad is well known in Maine, but is probably of New Brunswick origin. The following variant of lines in the fourth stanza was picked up by W. H. Hardy, of Brewer, Maine, in New York City from one who had heard a guide singing it in the Rangeley Lake region in the extreme western part of Maine:

> O the bears and the owls
> With their terrifying growls
> They do disturb my nightly rest.

Cf. "The Cowboy's Life," in Lomax's *Cowboy Songs*, pp. 20 f.

B, though somewhat different from A, is evidently related. It was printed as a broadside by Andrews, New York City, as "Composed and Written by Geo. W. Stace, La Crosse Valley, Wis." Later the same text was printed in Henry de Marsan's *Comic and Sentimental Singer's Journal*, No. 93, I, 708, as "Composed and Written by Geo. W. Stage." DeMarsan was Andrews's successor in business.

A

1   The lumberman's life
Is a wearisome one,
But some say 't is free from all care;
With the ringing of an ax
From daylight until dark
In the middle of some forest you'll hear.

2   At night we come in
To our camps bleak and cold,
And till nine in the evening we play;
And through broken slumbers
We do pass
All the cold winter nights away.

3   At three in the morning
The cook he does rise up,
Saying, "Turn out, my boys, 't is day."
And as soon as the morning
Star does appear
To the greenwoods we must away.

4   Transported are we are
From the maiden so fair
On the banks of the bushisle[1] stream
And the wolves and the owls
With their terrifying howls
They disturb us of our nightly dream.

5   Transported are we are
From the bottle and the glass
And the friends that we left far behind;
There is no one comes here
For to wipe away a tear
When sorrow fills our troubled mind.

6   Now the spring is coming on
And our hardship's just begun,
And the water it is piercing cold;
With our clothes dripping wet,
And our limbs nearly froze,
And our peavies we scarce can hold.

[1] So in the MS.

7   Over rocks, shoals, and strands
         Gives employment to all hands,
While our well-banded craft we do steer;
        And the rapids we do run
        They do seem to us like fun;
We avoid all slavish [1] fear.

8   You may boast of your farms,[2]
        But the lumberman's charms
Do far more exceed them all.
        I'll enjoy my true love's heart
        Until death it does us part
Let her riches be great or small.

B

A SHANTYMAN'S LIFE

1   Oh, a Shantyman's life is a weary one,
        Though some call it free from care,
It's wielding the axe, from morning till night,
        Midst the forest dark and drear.
A lying in the shanty, bleak and cold,
        Where the stormy winds do blow;
And as soon as the morning stars appear,
        To the wild-wood we must go.

[1] *Slaverage* in original.
[2] Original has "farmers" rhyming with "charm."

Transported we are, from the pretty maidens fair
  On the banks of Black River stream,
Where the wolves, and the owls, with their terrify-
    ing howls,
  Disturb our nightly dreams

2   At two o'clock, our early cook,
      Calls out, 't is the break of day.
    In broken slumbers, we do pass,
      The long winter nights away.
    Had we Ale, Wine or Beer, our spirits to cheer,
      Whilst in the desert wild,
    Or a glass of any thown, whilst in the woods alone,
      'T would shorten our long exile,
    But we've parted from the glass, and the smiling
        lovely lass,
      All pleasures left behind;
    No kind friends near, to wipe the falling tear,
      When sorrow fills the troubled mind.

3   When spring comes in, double hardships begin,
      And the waters, piercing cold,
    Dripping wet our clothes,[1] our limbs are almost
        froze,
      To our oars, we can scarcely hold,
    But the rocks, shoals, and sands, give employment
        to all hands,
      Our well-bended raft to steer,
    And the rapids, that we run,
      To us they are but fun,
    Void of all slavish fear.

---

[1] Misprinted "chothes" in the broadside.

Now a shanty-boy, I do love the best,
And I never will deny the same,
   For his heart scorneth those conceity beaus,
That call it a disgraceful name.

4   It makes me, indeed, my very heart to bleed,
   To see the danger, he daily does stand,
But all this he will repay, in some future happy day,
   When joined in wedlock band.
All rafting he'll give o'er, and anchor safe on shore,
   Lead a quiet and sober life,
Never more will he roam, from his peaceful, happy
     home,
   But he'll marry him a pretty little wife.

The Lumberman in Town

SUNG by Dyer, a mill-hand, of East Eddington, Maine, in 1901, and taken down by W. H. Hardy, of Brewer, Maine.

1   When the lumberman comes down,
Ev'ry pocket bears a crown,
And he wa-a-anders some pretty girl to find.
If she is not too sly, with her dark and rolling eye,
   The lumberman is pleased in his mind,
   The lumberman is pleased in his mind.

2   The landlady comes in,
She is dressed so neat and trim,
She looks just like an ev-en-in' star;
She's ready to wait on him, if she finds he's in good
      trim,
   Chalk him down for two to one at the bar,
   Chalk him down for two to one at the bar.

3   The lumberman goes on
Till his earnt money's all spent and gone,
Then the landlady begins to frown.
With her dark and rolling eye, this will always be
      her cry;
   "Lumberman, it is time that you were gone,
   Lumberman, it is time that you were gone."

4   She gives him to understand
There's a boat to be a-manned,
And away up the river he must go:
Good liquor and a song, it's go hitch your horses on;
   Bid adieu to the girls of St. John,
   Bid adieu to the girls of St. John.

5 To the woods he will go,
With his heart so full of woe,
And he wa-a-anders from tree after tree,
Till six months have gone and past, he forgets it all
   at last:
    "It is time I should have another spree,
    It is time I should have another spree."

6 When old age does him alarm,
He will settle on a farm,
And he'll find some young girl to be his wife;
But to his sad mistake, she false love to him will
   make,
    And kind death will cut the tender threads of life,
    And kind death will cut the tender threads of life.

Mell Whitten

TAKEN down for the editor by a former student in the University of Maine, 1916. "White-headed Bob" is supposed to be the principal author, with Heyward and Marshall assisting.

1   In the month of October eighteen eighty-two,
Mell Whitten from Bangor he started a crew.
A crew of young fellows with him he did take,
And he landed them safely upon Moosehead Lake.
    Sing fol-de-diddle, darow
    Li-turrol-o-day.

2   When he arrived at the North West Carry,
There he met our boss and we got on a spree.
We put up our store house and struck for the camp;
But we lost one of our bushmen all on that wild
        tramp.
    Sing fol-de-diddle, darow
    Li-turrol-o-day.

3   When we got there the boss he did say:
"There's axes to grind and there's no time for stay,
For next Monday morning to the woods you must
        go,
And it's forty-five spruce every day you must
        throw.
    Sing fol-de-diddle, darow
    Li-turrol-o-day.

4   They hired an Englishman in Bangor, Maine
To go up and swamp, Bill Williams by name.
When he got there, "I'm a chopper," says he;
But the best he could do was to lodge every tree.
    Sing fol-de-diddle, darow
    Li-turrol-o-day.

5   Says Whitten to Williams, "I know what I'll do,
I'll send you to Suncook with bold Heehan too;
So pack up your dunnage and the tote road you
       take,
For I know that McMannan will find you a mate."
    Sing fol-de-diddle, darow
    Li-turrol-o-day.

6   They hired a cook, from Orneville came he,
And a dirtier old cook you never did see.
Raw beans and cold dough he would give us to eat,
And about once a week a big feed of corned beef.
    Sing fol-de-diddle, darow
    Li-turrol-o-day.

7   They bought an alarm clock, this cook for to wake.
He sometimes would n't hear it until it was late;
And then he'd get up in a terrible stew.
Raw beans and cold dough he would feed to the
       crew.
    Sing fol-de-diddle, darow
    Li-turrol-o-day.

8   About six in the morning the cook he would shout:
"Come bullies, come bullies, come bullies, roll out."

If we would n't mind him and back we would lay,
The boss would sing out: "Are you going to sleep
    all day."
    Sing fol-de-diddle, darow
    Li-turrol-o-day.

9   About twelve at noon, when the sky it was clear,
All through the woods would be, "Luncheon,"
    you'd hear.
But when you got there, 't was all you could see
Was a dirty old cook and a lousy cookee.
    Sing fol-de-diddle, darow
    Li-turrol-o-day.

10   About six in the morning for the camp we would
    steer,
"I board the grindstone" was all you could hear.
"I board the grindstone," for the turns they would
    fight,
And they'd keep that old grindstone a-whirling all
    night.
    Sing fol-de-diddle, darow
    Li-turrol-o-day.

11   And now to conclude, and to finish my song.
'T was composed upon Sunday, I hope it's not
    wrong.
There was Heyward the chopper,
And white-headed Bob, and Marshall the sled-
    tender
Who would n't bark a log.
    Sing fol-de-diddle, darow
    Li-turrol-o-day.

Peter Ambelay

THERE are several variants of this ballad as sung in Maine. W. R. Mackenzie in *The Quest of the Ballad* (p. *35*) quotes from memory two lines sung to him during his childhood in Nova Scotia by Edward Langille, a cobbler, of River John, Nova Scotia:

O my name is Peter Ambelay, as you shall understand.
My home is in Prince Edward Island, down by the ocean strand.

Langille is now dead, and Professor Mackenzie informs the editor that he has not found the rest of the ballad.

A

"PETER AMERLY," *sung by a lumberjack in Maine and taken down for the editor, in 1916, by a student in the University of Maine. Stanza 10 is from "Mary Hamilton" (Child, No. 173, A 15, B 17).*

1   My name is Peter Amerly,
      As you may understand,
    Born on Prince Edward Island
      Close by the ocean strand.

2   In eighteen hundred eighty-two,
      When the flowers were in brilliant hue,
    I sailed away from my native land
      My fortune to pursue.

3   I landed in New Brunswick,
      That lumbering countteree;
    I hired to work in the lumber woods
      In the North West Merrimachi.

4   I hired to work in the lumber woods,
      Where they cut those tall spruce down;
    And 't was loading two sleds on a yard
      I received a mortal wound.

5   Here's adieu unto Prince Edward's Isle,
      That garden in the sea;
    No more I'll walk its flowery banks
      To enjoy a summer's breeze.

6   No more I'll watch those gallant ships,
      As they go sailing by,
    With the streamers floating in the breeze
      Far above the canvas high.

7   Here's adieu unto my father;
      'T was him who sent me here;
    I thought he used me most unkind,
      His treatments were severe.

8   It is not right to press a boy
      Or to try and keep him down;
    For it ofttimes drives him from his house
      When he is far too young.

9   Here's adieu unto my greater friend,
      I mean my mother dear.
    She raised a son, who fell as soon
      As he left his mother's care.

10   For little did my mother know,
      When she sung lullaby
    What countries I might travel in,
      Or what death I might die.

11 There's danger on the ocean,
    Where the waves roll mountain high;
    There's danger on the battlefield,
    Where the angry bullets fly.

12 There's danger in the lumberwoods,
    For death lurks even there;
    And I have fell a victim now
    Unto this monster's snare.

13 And when I'm dead and gone to rest,
    There's one thing more I crave,
    That the kind heavenly Father
    May bless my peaceful grave;

14 For it's in the village of Bois Town
    My mouldering corpse they'll lay,
    To wait the Saviour's calling
    Until that great Judgment Day.

B

"PETER EMELY," *sung by Murray of Holden, Maine, March, 1914. Taken down by W. M. Hardy. Murray, an expert woodsman, was from the Provinces, and may have brought this ballad with him.*

1   My name is Peter Emely,
    As you may understand;
    I belong to Prince Edward Island
    Close by the native shore.

2   In eighteen eighty-eight,
      When the flowers were a brilliant hue,
    I left my native country
      My fortune to pursue.

3   When I landed in New Brunswick,
      In that lumbering counteree,
    I hired to work in the lumber woods,
      Which proved my destiny.

4   .   .   .   .   .

      .   .   .   .   .
    Whilst loading two sleds from the yard,
      I received my deathly wound.

5   There is danger in the ocean,
      When the seas roll mountain high;
    There is danger on the battlefield,
      Where the angry bullets fly;

6   There is danger in the lumber woods
      And death lies solemn there,
    And I have fallen a victim
      Unto my monster snare.

7   Here's adieu [1] unto my father
      'T is him who drove me here;
    I could not put up with him,
      His treatment drove me here.

---

[1] The expression "Here's adieu, etc." is always sung as if it were "Here's a due against my father," and appears to be conceived as a curse upon the father. It is sung very sternly.

8 It is not right to press a boy
  Or try to keep him down;
 It ofttimes makes him leave his home
  When he is far too young.

9 There's adieu unto my nearer friend,
  That is my mother dear;
 She had reared a son of hers,
  All in her tender care.

10 And little did my mama think,
  When she sung sweet lullaby,
 What country I might travel in
  Or the death that I might die.

11 Here's adieu unto those Island girls,
  Those Island girls so true,

  . . . . .

   . . . . .

12 No more I'll walk those flowery banks
  To see those ships pass by
 And steamers floating in the breeze,
  With canvas half-mast high.

13 In the city of Boiestown
  Where my mouldering bones do lie

  . . . . .

   . . . . .

C

*"*Peter Emberlie,*" printed in* The Sportsman, *a Maine pub-
lication which died "many years ago." It was sent to the paper
by a reader who wished "to perpetuate the songs sung among
the lumbermen of Maine."*

1   My name is Peter Emberlie
     As you may understand,
  I was born in Prince Edward Island
     Down by the ocean strand.

2   In Eighteen Hundred and Eighty
     When the flowers were in their bloom
  I left my native country
     My fortune to pursue.

3   I landed in New Brunswick
     That lumbering counter-ee
  I hired to work in the lumber woods
     Which proved my destiny.

4   I hired to work in the lumber woods
     To cut the spruce logs down.
  While loading two sleds from the yard
     I received my deathly wound.

5   There is danger on the dark blue sea
     Where the waves roll mountain high;
  There is danger on the battlefield
     Where the angry bullets fly;

6 There is danger in the lumber woods
  Where death lurks silent there,
 And I have fell a victim
  All to its monstrous snare.

7 Here's adieu unto you, Father,
  'T was you that drove me here,
 I could not well agree with you,
  Your treatment was severe.

8 A man should never force a boy
  Or try to keep him down,
 For it often drives him from his home
  When he is far too young.

9 Here's adieu unto a better friend —
  I mean my mother dear,
 Little did I think I would fall a victim
  When I left her tender care.

10 It's little did my mother know
  When she sung sweet lullaby,
 In what country I would end my days
  Or what death I might die.

11 Here's adieu to Prince Edward Island
  That garden in the seas;
 No more I'll roam it's flowery banks
  To enjoy a summer breeze.

12 No more I'll watch those gallant ships
  As they go sailing by
 With colors flying gaily,
  Above their canvas high.

The Days in Old Penobscot Stream

TEXT written from memory by a lumberjack, Orono, Maine, 1916.

1   Out in Boston City
　　In the middle of July,
　When five and twenty lumberjacks
　　To the loved ones bid good-by,

2 . We landed in Suhomuck,
　　All feeling pretty mean;
　But on we went and pitched our tent
　　On old Penobscot stream.

3   Our work is cutting dry kye,
　　To clear a right of way.
　The hours were long, but we were strong
　　And work hard day by day.

4   The Suhomuck once was beautiful,
　　Its mountains and scenery grand;
　The fish that's in the river
　　Is the best that's in the land.

5   The work went rolling nicely
　　For just about one week,
　And somewhere in Suhomuck
　　The sky began to leak.

6   For eating we had plenty
      Of those grand and glorious beans,
    Lots of ham behind the dam,
      On old Penobscot stream.

7   Our boss he was a good fellow,
      Our cook was a cockereen;
    We never forget the boys
      We left in old Penobscot stream.

8   Now the days are all gone past,
      It seems but all a dream.
    We'll never forget the friends
      We left in old Penobscot stream.

OLD BALLADS AND OTHER PIECES

The Twa Sisters

TAKEN down by H. M. R., in Calais, Maine, and printed by Barry, with another version, with the music, in the *Journal of American Folk-Lore*, 1905, XVIII, 130–132. This ballad is incomplete; but corresponds in plot, except in minor details, to the first part of "The Twa Sisters," No. 10, in Child's collection of *English and Scottish Popular Ballads*. The complete ballad is probably not yet extinct as tradition in the British Isles. It has been found, Child affirms, in England, Scotland, Wales, and Ireland. There are also Danish, Icelandic, Norwegian, Färöe, and Swedish versions. In all complete and uncorrupted forms of the ballad, according to Child, "either some part of the body of the drowned girl is taken to furnish a musical instrument, a harp or a viol, or the instrument is wholly made from the body." The frame of the harp, for instance, is made of the breast-bone and the pins of the finger joints. In the more felicitous version, the girl's lover takes three locks of her yellow hair with which to string his harp.

Two variants and a fragment are printed by Belden, *Journal of American Folk-Lore*, 1906, XIX, 233–235. For other American texts, see Campbell and Sharp, *English Folk Songs from the Southern Appalachians*, pp. 16–19; Sharp, *Folk-Songs of English Origin*, 2d Series, pp. 18–21; Cox, *The School Journal and Educator* (West Virginia), 1916, XLIV, 428, 441–442; Child, I, 137; Pound, *American Ballads and Songs* [1922], pp. 11–13.

1   There was a man lived in the West,
      Bow down, bow down,
    There was a man lived in the West, —
      The bow is bent to me, —
    There was a man lived in the West,
    He loved his youngest daughter best.
      Prove true, prove true,
      Oh, my love, prove true to me!

2 One day he gave her a beaver hat,
   Her sister, she did not like that.

3 As they were walking on the green,
   To see their father's ships come in,

4 As they were walking on the wharf,
   Her sister, she did push her off.

5 "Oh, dear sister, give me your hand,
   And you shall have my house and land!"

6 "No, I will not give you my hand,
   But I will have your house and land."

7 Sometimes she sank, sometimes she swam,
   Until she came to a miller's dam.

8 The miller he put in his hook,
   And fished her out by her petticoat.

9 He stripped her off from toe to chin,
   And then he threw her in agin.

10 Sometimes she sunk, sometimes she swum,
   Until she came to her long home.

11 Her sister was hanged for her sake,
   And the miller, he burned at the stake.

The following stanzas, which I quote in order to complete the story, are from B of "The Twa Sisters" in Child's collection.

19 The miller quickly drew the dam,
   And there he found a drownd woman.

20 You coudna see her yallow hair
   For gold and pearle that were so rare.

21   You coudna see her middle sma
        For gouden girdle that was sae braw.

22   You coudna see her fingers white,
        For gouden rings that was sae gryte.

23   An by there came a harper fine,
        That harped to the king at dine.

24   When he did look that lady upon,
        He sighd and made a heavy moan.

25   He's taen three locks o her yallow hair,
        An wi them strung his harp sae fair.

26   The first tune he did play and sing,
        Was, "Farewell to my father the king."

27   The nextin tune that he played syne,
        Was, "Farewell to my mother the queen."

28   The lasten tune that he playd then,
        Was, "Wae to my sister, fair Ellen."

Strawberry Lane

PRINTED by Kittredge in the *Journal of American Folk-Lore*, 1917, XXX, 284–285, with the tune; communicated in 1914 by Mr. E. Russell Davis, as remembered by his mother and himself from the singing of his grandfather, Mr. William Henry Banks (born 1834), a vessel-owner of Maine. It is a variant of "The Elfin Knight" (Child, No. 2). The ballad is well known in England and in many parts of this country, as far south as Texas and as far west as California (see the *Journal* for details).

1   As I was a-walking up Strawberry Lane, —
      Every rose grows merry and fine, —
    I chanced for to meet a pretty, fair maid,
      Who wanted to be[1] a true-lover of mine.

2   "You'll have for to make me a cambric shirt, —
      Every rose grows merry and fine, —
    And every stitch must be finicle work,
      Before you can be a true-lover of mine.

3   "You'll have for to wash it in a deep well, —
      Every rose grows merry and fine, —
    Where water never was nor rain ever fell,
      Before you can be a true-lover of mine."

The man goes on to make several more conditions. Finally the girl turns on him thus: —

4   "Now, since you have been so hard with me, —
      Every rose grows merry and fine, —
    Perhaps I can be as hard with thee,
      Before you can be a true-lover of mine.

[1] Or "said she would be."

5 "You'll have for to buy me an acre of ground, —
  Every rose grows merry and fine, —

 . . . . .

  Before you can be a true-lover of mine.

6 "You'll have for to plough it with a deer's horn, —
  Every rose grows merry and fine, —
And plant it all over with one grain of corn,
  Before you can be a true-lover of mine.

7 "You'll have for to thrash it in an eggshell, —
  Every rose grows merry and fine, —
And bring it to market in a thimble,[1]
  Before you can be a true-lover of mine."

[1] Or "And take it to market where man never dwelled."

Andrew Martine

As printed by Barry, *Journal of American Folk-Lore*, 1905, XVIII, 302–303, from a text contributed to the *Boston Transcript* by A. C. A., who states: "I can give the song, as I heard it sung many years ago in Portland, Maine, by Eliza Ostinelli, daughter of Ostinelli, the musician,—she afterward went to Italy, where she married, and was known as Mme. Biscaccianti, 'The American Thrush.'"

See Child's *English and Scottish Popular Ballads*, No. 250 A ("Henry Martyn") and E ("Andrew Bartin"), p. 553 (Sargent-Kittredge edition). "Andrew Martine" is evidently a shorter and inferior variant of E. All have sprung from "Sir Andrew Barton" (Child, No. 167); an important version from Kentucky, which shows this connection clearly, is printed by Belden, *Journal*, XXV, 171–173. For the music, see Barry, *Journal of American Folk-Lore*, 1905, XVIII, 135 ("sung over fifty years ago").

1   There dwelt three brothers in merry Scotland,
       Three brothers there dwelt there, three,
   And they did cast lots to see which one
       Should go robbing upon the salt sea,
       Should go robbing upon the salt sea.

2   The lot it fell upon Andrew Martine
       The youngest of the three,
   That he should go robbing upon the salt sea,
       To support his three brothers and he.

3   "Oh, who are you?" said Andrew Martine,
       "Who are you that comes tossing so high?"
   "I am a brave ship from merry England,
       Will you please for to let me pass by?"

4   "Oh, no, oh no!" said Andrew Martine,
      "Oh no, that never can be!
   Your ship and your cargo we'll all take away,
      And your bodies give to the salt sea!"

5   The news it came to merry England,
      And to King George's ears,
   And he did fit out a nice little band,
      For to catch this Andrew Martine.

6   "Oh, who are you?" said Captain Charles Stuart,
      "Who are you that comes tossing so high?"
   "I am a brave ship from merry Scotland,
      Will you please for to let me pass by?"

7   "Oh, no, oh no!" said Captain Charles Stuart,
      "Oh, no that never can be!
   Your ship and your cargo we'll all take away,
      And your bodies give to the salt sea."

8   They fought and fought, and fought again,
      Until the light did appear,
   And where was Andrew, and all his brave crew?
      Their bodies were in the salt sea.

Mary Aclon

RECITED by J. F. Shedd of Mattawamkeag, Maine, and taken down
by the editor, 1916. It was afterward sung by Mr. Shedd and
his daughter. Mr. Shedd, who was over seventy years old, had
taught it to his daughter when she was a little girl. Neither had
seen a written or printed copy.

When he recited Mr. Shedd gave:

There I met with a charming young creature.

When he sang it he said:

There I met with the squire's young daughter.

This last rendering was probably due to the anticipation of the
fourth line following which is:

And now for the squire's young daughter.

Mr. Shedd said that the line given first by recital was the correct
one.

1   Come all you young lovers draw near,
    And the truth unto you I'll unfold.
  In sorrow I am left here bewailing;
    No comfort have I to behold.

2   Three months in a sad situation,
    Confined in cold irons 't is true;
  And for nothing but loving a fair one
    I fear I must bid you adieu.

3   It was down by a green shady harbor,
    Where the flowers were blooming so gay;
  There I met with a charming young creature;
    She exceeded the fair Queen of May.

4 When Venus discovered her beauty,
   False Cupid he did me annoy.
   And now for the squire's young daughter
   In cold chains in prison I lie.

5 But Mary, being constant and loyal,
   Straightway to my trial did come.
   My parents were weeping, forlorning;
   She said, "Now I will protect you, dear son."

6 She was dressed like some lady of honor,
   The best of gold robes she did wear:
   And all the great judges were surprised,
   And all the grand jury did stare.

7 She kindly saluted those nobles
   And unto them she did say:
   "In case that he loved a fair female,
   Why should he be banished away?"

8 For it is seven long years we've been courting;
   I own that I gave him my heart,
   And there's nothing but death that can ease me,
   If Jamie and I have to part.

9 And now for to make a conclusion,
   And thanks to the powers above!
   And likewise to young Mary Aclon,
   For she wears the armor of love!

10 Her father, he thought to transport me
   Far away from my own country,
   But she has released me from bondage
   And set me at sweet liberty.

11 And now we are married and happy,
  Our fortunes on both sides paid down;
  Our parents are likewise contented,
  Although it caused many a frown.

12 We dwell on the banks of the Shannon
  In love and in sweet unity,
  And I think of the squire's young daughter,
  And so loyal she has proved to me!

In Blithe and Bonnie Fair Scotland

TAKEN down for the editor by Miss Chadburne of Mattawam-keag, Maine, 1916, from the singing of Frank Fowler, lumber-jack. This ballad is known in English broadsides as "The Paisley Officer."

1   In blithe and bonnie Scotland,
     Where blue bells there do grow,
   There lived a fair and comely maiden
     Down in the valley low,

2   A-herding there her father's flock
     Down by the river side.
   Although her lot in life was low,
     She was called the village pride.

3   An officer down from Peasley town
     A-hunting came that way.
   He hunted round those lowland shades
     Where Mary's cot doth lay.

4   With a long and loving eye he cast
     Upon her form so fair,
   And wondered how so fair a plum
     Had grown and flourished there.

5   And then each day he came
     That way and her a visit paid,
   Until at length he gained the heart
     Of this fair village dame.

6   Together they roamed o'er hill and dale
    And in the valleys fair,
  And much he wondered so fair a flower
    Could bloom and flourish there.

7   Young Henry he came in one day,
    His face was decked with woe:
  "Say Mary, lovely Mary,
    'Tis from you I must go."

8   "Our regiment they have got the route,
    And I've received command.
  So fare you well, you lowland shades
    For India's burning sands."

9   "O Henry, dearest Henry,
    It grieves me to the heart!
  I wish we might get married
    The night before we part.

10   "I wish I was your wedded wife;
    'T would be my heart's desire.
  Your servant boy so nice I'd be,
    Disguised in man's attire."

11   As they marched up through Peasley town,
    'T was much they wondered there
  All for to see this young recruit
    So gentle and so fair.

12   The ladies fell in love with her,
    As she marched on parade;
  But little they think a soldier's coat
    Could conceal so fair a maid.

13   They quickly crossed the ocean
        For India's burning shore;
    Hard for any tongue to tell
        What Mary did endure.

14   When she found her strength was gone,
        Her woe she strove to hide,
    And turning round with a pleasant smile,
        Saw Henry by her side.

15   The battle it was raging on;
        A spear soon pierced his side:
    He never flinched nor left his post,
        But where he fell, he died.

16   She drew him from the bloody field
        And in her arms she pressed,
    And as she sought to heal his wound,
        A ball passed through her breast.

17   "I fear you're deeply wounded,"
        Young Henry he did say;
    "I fear you're deeply wounded;
        Your face is like the clay.

18   "When first since I saw your face,
        'T was you I did adore."
    They closed their eyes, no more to rise,
        On India's burning shore.

Lowlands Low

Sung by Murray, in Holden, Maine, 1914, and taken down by W. M. Hardy. The title was given by Murray after some groping in his memory. The song, however, is evidently an alteration of "The Lowlands of Holland" (see Herd, *Ancient and Modern Scottish Songs*, 1776, II, 2 ff.). Other forms may be found in Logan, *A Pedlar's Pack of Ballads and Songs*, pp. 22 ff. (see Child, *English and Scottish Popular Ballads*, II, 317; V, 229); Sharp, *One Hundred English Folksongs*, pp. 54–55 (cf. p. xxvii); Herbert Hughes, *Irish Country Songs*, II, 70 ff.; and in broadsides (as H. Such, No. 236).

1   It's when we were married
      And lay on our bed,
  Up stepped a bold sea-captain
      And stood at my bed-head,

2   Saying, "Arise, arise, ye married man,
      And come along with me
  To the Lowlands of Holland
      To fight your enemy."

  Chorus. — My curse rest on that captain
      That parted my love and me.

3   The Lowlands is a cold place,
      And a place where they grow no green,
  Neither flowers nor habitations
      For a stranger to dwell in.

4   .   .   .   .   .
    .   .   .   .   .
  But the money is as plenty
      As the leaves upon the tree.

Chorus. — My curse rest on that captain
    That parted my love and me.

5   There will ne'er a sash go round my waist
      Nor a comb go in my hair,
    Neither fire, coal, nor candlelight
      To show my beauty fair.

Chorus. — My curse rest on that captain
    That parted my love and me.

6   And neither will I married be
      Until the day I dee,
    Since stormy winds and cruel waves
      Have parted my love from me.

Chorus. — My curse rest on that captain
    That sailed the stormy seas.

The Prentice Boy's Love for Mary

Sung by J. F. Shedd, Mattawamkeag, Maine, and written down by the editor, 1916. This is the well-known ballad of "The Sheffield Apprentice," common in broadsides and still orally circulated in England and Scotland as well as in this country. See W. C. Ford, *Massachusetts Broadsides*, No. 3307; Perrow, *Journal of American Folk-Lore*, XXVIII, 164 (cf. XXXII, 499); Shearin and Coombs, *Syllabus of Kentucky Folk-Songs*, p. 11; Shearin, *The Sewanee Review*, July, 1911; Campbell and Sharp, *English Folk Songs from the Southern Appalachians*, pp. 278–280; *The Forget Me Not Songster*, p. 244; *Elton's Songs and Melodies for the Multitude*, pp. 318–319; broadside, H. de Marsan, New York, List 9, No. 91.

A ballad, called "Sheffield," sung in the Cumberland mountains, tells the same story as ours but differs in details: the rich lady comes from Ireland instead of Holland, and the Prentice has plighted his troth to Polly Girl instead of to Mary. The lines are shorter and the wording differs considerably, but the plot is identical.

1   I was brought up in Sheffield,
        Not of a high degree;
    My parents they adored on me,
        They had no other child but me.

2   I roamed with much pleasure
        Where e'er my fancy led,
    Till I was bound a prentice boy;
        Then all my hopes were fled.

3   I did not like my master,
     He did not use me well;
  I formed a resolution
     Not long with him to dwell.

4   Unknown to my dear parents,
     I quickly ran away
  And steered my course for London;
     All wretched be that day!

5   A handsome young lady
     From Holland was there;
  She offered me great wages
     To serve her for one year.

6   Induced by her promises,
     I quickly did agree
  To go and live in Holland,
     Which proved my destiny.

7   I had not been in Holland
     Past months two or three,
  Before my new mistress
     Grew very fond of me.

8   She said her gold and her silver,
     Her houses and rich land,
  If I'd consent to marry her,
     Should be at my command.

9   I said, "Your honor'd lady,
     I could not love you both,
  For lately I have promised
     And made a solemn oath

10   "To marry none but Mary,
     Your charming kitchen maid.
    Excuse me, my dear mistress,
     She has my heart betrayed."

11   Then in an angry humor
     Away from me she ran,
    Resolved to be revenged
     Before it was ere long.

12   She being so perplexed
     That she could not be my wife,
    She then did seek a project
     To take away my life.

13   One day as we were walking
     All in the garden gay,
    The flowers they were blooming,
     Delightfully in May,

14   A gold ring from her finger,
     As I was passing by,
    She slipped into my pocket;
     And for it I must die.

15   My mistress swore I'd robbed her;
     Then quickly I was brought
    Before a grave old justice
     To answer for my fault.

16   Long time I pleaded innocent,
     But it was of no avail;
    She swore so hard against me
     That I was put in jail.

17 Now as the 'sizes
        Are drawing to a close,
    Presently the judge
        Will sentence on me pass.

18 At the close of my confinement
        They'll hang me to a tree.
    Adieu to my poor mistress,
        For she has ruined me.

19 Now all you young people,
        Who my wretched fate do see,
    Don't glory in my downfall;
        I pray you pity me.

20 Knowing I am innocent,
        I bid this world adieu.
    Adieu to my poor Mary dear!
        I die for loving you.

Fair Charlotte

Sung to the editor by Frank Fowler, and taken down by Miss Chadburne, a University student, both in Mattawamkeag, Maine, 1916. Phillips Barry, who has traced the history of this song for nearly a hundred years, ascribes it to William Carter, who was a blind poet of Bensontown, Vermont, 1835 (*Journal of American Folk-Lore*, XXV, 156–158). Mr. Reid, Bangor, Maine, a former woodsman, says that his father taught him this song when he was six or seven years old, and that his father had known it a long time. Mr. Reid, I judge, was at the time over sixty years old. Many versions of this song have been collected from all over the country.

1   Young Charlotte dwelt by the mountain side
     In a rude and lonely spot;
   There was no house for three miles round
     Except her father's cot.

2   And yet on many a wintry eve
     Young swain would gather there;
   For her father kept a social abode,
     And she was very fair.

3   He liked to see his daughter dressed
     Just like a city belle;
   For she was the only child he had,
     And he loved his daughter well.

4   Her hair was black as raven's wing,
     And her skin like lilies fair,
   And her teeth were like the pearls so white:
     Few with her could compare.

5   At the village inn fifteen miles off
      There's a merry ball tonight.
    Although the air is freezing cold,
      Our hearts are warm and light.

6   How eager was her restless gaze
      Till a well known voice she did hear
    And driving up to the cottage door
      Charles Leslie did appear.

7   "O daughter dear," the mother said,
      "This blanket around you fold,
    For it is a dreadful night abroad,
      You'll catch your death of cold."

8   "Oh nay! Oh nay!" young Charlotte said,
      And she laughed like a gypsy queen:
    "To ride in blankets muffled up
      I never would be seen.

9   "My silken cloak is quite enough,
      You know 't is lined throughout;
    Besides I have a silken shawl
      My face to tie about."

10   Her gloves and bonnet being on,
      She jumped into the sleigh,
    And away they rode to the mountain-side
      And over the hills away.

11   There is music in the sound of merry bells,
      As over the hills they go.
    What a reeking wake those runners make,
      As they bite the frosty snow!

12   Then away they rode so silent
       Till five cold long miles were past,
    When Charles with these few frozen words
       The silence broke at last:

13   "Such a night as this I never knew;
       My reins I scarce can hold."
    Young Charlotte exclaimed with a feeble voice,
       "I am exceeding cold."

14   He cracked his whip and he urged his steed
       Much faster than before,
    Until at length five more cold miles
       In silence was passed o'er.

15   "Oh! how fast the freezing ice.
       Dost gather on my brow."
    Young Charlotte exclaimed with a feeble voice,
       "I am growing warmer now."

16   Then away they rode through the frosty air
       And by the cold starlight,
    Until at length the village inn
       And ball room hove in sight.

17   They reached the inn, and Charles sprang out
       And gave his hand to her.
    "Why sit you there like a monument
       That hath no power to stir?"

18   He asked her once, he asked her twice;
       But she said not a word;
    He asked her for her hand again,
       But still she never stirred.

19 He tore the muffler from her face,
And the cold stars on her shone,
And quickly in the lighted hall
Her lifeless form was borne.

20 They tried every means they could
Her life for to restore;
But Charlotte was a frozen corpse
And never could speak more.

21 He sat himself down by her side,
And the bitter tears did flow;
He said, "My dear intended bride
I never more shall know."

22 He threw his arms around her neck
And kissed her marble brow,
And his thoughts went back to the place
Where she said, "I'm growing warmer now."

23 He bore her back into the sleigh
And with her he rode home,
And when he reached her father's house,
Oh! how her parents mourned!

24 They mourned the loss of their daughter dear,
And Charles mourned o'er his doom,
Until at length his heart had broke:
Now they slumber in one tomb.

The Zebra Dunn

TEXT as recited by a lumberjack at Plaster Rock region, New Brunswick, Canada. He learned it in the "North West." Taken down by T. A. Madison, Kingman, Maine, 1917. It is evidently an inferior variant of "The Zebra Dunn" in Lomax's *Cowboy Songs*, pp. 154–157.

1   We were camped out on the plain,
    At the head of the Commisson,
When along came a stranger,
    Who wanted to argue some.

2   Such an educated fellow,
    His words just came in herds;
He astonished all them cowboys
    With his jaw-breaking words.

3   We thought he was a tenderfoot,
    Just escaped from town,
And we soon began to plan on
    How we could have some fun.

4   We asked about his breakfast:
    He had n't had a snip;
So we opened the chick-box
    And told him to help himself.

5   He took a plate of beans and
    Then some beer and bread,
And then began to tell us
    Foreign knights and queens;

6   And about the Spanish War
     And fighting upon the sea,
   With guns as big as steers
     And ramrods as big as trees.

7   He talked about the weather,
     Ropes, skins and things;
   He did n't seem to know much
     Of working on the range.

8   He just kept blowing his bazoo
     Till he made the boys all sick;
   And we just began to plan
     Just how to turn the trick.

9   He said he was on his way
     To strike the Seven D's;
   He said he 's lost his job
     Down close to the Santa Fe.

10   Some trouble with the boss —
     He did n't give the cause;
   He said he would like to have
     A nice, fresh, fat saddle horse.

11   This tickled the boys all over,
     And laughed down in their sleeves:
   "Yes, we will give you a horse
     As fresh and fat as you please."

12   So Shorty grabbed his lariat
     And roped the Zebra Dunn,
   And turned him over to the stranger,
     And we waited to see the fun.

13   Now old Dunn was a rocky outlaw,
       And he had grown powerful wild:
    He would paw the white out of the moon,
       Every jump for a mile.

14   Old Dunny stood plum still,
       Not seeming to know
    The stranger had him saddled
       And was picking up to go.

15   But when the stranger mounted,
       Old Dunny quit the earth,
    And travelled straight up
       For all he was worth.

16   Old Dunny booed and balled
       Just like a jersey calf;
    While the stranger began to quirt his flanks,
       And we began to laugh.

17   Old Dunny was standing on his head,
       Having wall-eyed fits,
    His hind feet perpendicular,
       His front ones in the bits.

18   But the stranger spurred him in the shoulders
       And whipped him as he turned,
    To show those flunkey punchers
       He was wolf of the world.

19   The boss was standing near-by
       Watching the fun;
    When the chap dismounted,
       He called him aside.

20   He said, "You need not leave this camp
     Unless you want to go;
   For I will give you a good long job
     And pay you with my dough.

21   "For if you can sling the catgut
     Like you ride old Dunn,
   You're the man I've been looking for
     Since the year one."

22   And he could throw the lariat
     And did n't do it slow;
   He could catch these fore-uns,
     Nine out of ten for a go.

23   And when the herd stampeded,
     He was Johnny-on-the-spot;
   He could get the herd to milling
     Like the stirring of the pot.

24   And there is one thing —
     And a sure thing too —
   That we've learned out of school,
     That all educated town-men are n't dam-fools.

The Dying Hobo

TAKEN down by L. A. Madison, an insurance agent, Kingman, Maine, 1914, who writes to the editor concerning the source: "I was in a lumber camp one evening four years past and there was one of the drifters of the world came in and recited the enclosed. I took it down in shorthand and when I got home I made a number of copies. He did not know who the author was, he picked it up in the northern lumber camps years ago." The song seems to be widely current. Professor J. H. Cox has found it in West Virginia.

1   Beside a western water tank
        One cold November day,
     Inside an empty box car
        A dying Hobo lay.

2   His partner stood beside him
        With low and drooping head
     And listened to the last words
        The dying Hobo said:

3   "I'm going to a better land,
        Where everything is bright,
     Where longnecks grow on bushes,
        And you sleep out every night;

4   "Where you do not have to work at all,
        Nor even change your socks,
     And little streams of alcohol
        Come twinkling down the rocks.

5   "Tell my sweetheart back in Denver
     That her fair face I no more will view;
  Tell her that I've jumped the fast freight
     And that I am going through.

6   "Tell her not to weep for me,
     In her eyes no tears must lurk,
  For I've gone to a better land,
     Where I won't have to work.

7   "Hark, I hear a whistle;
     I must catch her on the fly.
  Farewell, partner, it's not
     So hard to die."

8   The Hobo stopped, his head fell back;
     He had sung his last refrain.
  His partner swiped his hat and shoes
     And jumped the east-bound train.

Poor Old Horse

THIS song, of English origin but adapted by tradition to localities in Maine, was originally sung as part of a sailors' ceremony known as "the burial of the dead horse," a full account of which (with a text of the song) is given by Evelyn A. Melvill Richards in *Folk-Lore*, 1897, VIII, 281–283. For English texts (with tune) see also Bullen and Arnold, *Songs of Sea Labour*, No. 29, p. 25; Tozer, *Sailors' Songs*, 3d ed., No. 47, pp. 88–89; Whall, *Sea Songs and Shanties*, 4th ed., p. 119; Sharp, *English Folk-Chanteys*, No. 47, p. 52. It has often been used as a chantey. A fragmentary American text (with tune) may be found in Admiral Luce's *Naval Songs*, 2d ed., 1902, p. 224.

A somewhat similar song ("Poor Old Horse"), though quite distinct from this, is current in England. See Sharp, *One Hundred English Folksongs*, pp. xxxix, 196–197; Sharp, *English Folk Songs*, Selected Edition, II, xviii, 88–89; Sharp, *Folk-Songs of England*, IV, 16–17; Sharp and Marson, *Folk Songs from Somerset*, I, 54; Baring-Gould and Sharp, *English Folk-Songs for Schools*, No. 20, pp. 42–43. This is common in recent English broadsides (Forth, Pocklington; J. Livsey, Manchester, No. 240; Bebbington, Manchester, No. 140; Cadman, Manchester, No. 33), but the oldest printed text recorded is in a Boston, Massachusetts, broadside in the Isaiah Thomas collection (formed in 1813) in the library of the American Antiquarian Society (II, 120), "My Old Horse."

A

THE POOR OLD HORSE

THIS *little chantey, Professor L. M. Merrill (Orono, Maine) says, was taught him by his mother. He adds, "I understand that the song was once in general use along the New England coast." "Saccarappa" was the old name of Westbrook, Maine.*

1   "Old horse, old horse, how came you here?"
     "From Saccarap to Portland pier
     I've carted stone for many a year.

2   "Till, killed by blows and sore abuse,
     I was salted down for sailors' use.

3   "The sailors they do me despise;
     They turn me over and damn my eyes;

4   "Cut off my meat and pick my bones,
     And pitch the rest to Davy Jones."

B

THE POOR OLD MAN

From *Professor S. P. Chase, 1911, as sung to him "by Mr. Charles Creighton, of Thomaston, Maine, who was at one time a sailor and whose father was a sea-captain." A similar version was printed by Mr. Creighton's son, James A. Creighton, in* The Bowdoin Quill, *December, 1910, XIV, 230–231.*

1   There was an old man came riding along
         Chorus. — And we say so, and we know so.
     There was an old man came riding along
         Chorus. — With a poor old horse.

2   Says I, "Old man, your horse will die —
         Chorus. — And we say so, and we know so."
     Says I, "Old man, your horse will die —
         Chorus. — This poor old horse!"

3   "And if he dies, we'll tan his hide —
         Chorus. — And we say so, and we know so.
     And if he lives, we'll take a ride —
         Chorus. — This poor old horse!"

4   From Saccarapp to Portland Pier
      Chorus. — And we say so, and we know so.
      He 's carted rock for many a year —
      Chorus. — This poor old horse!

5   And now worn out with sore abuse,
      Chorus. — And we say so, and we know so.
      Salted down for sailors' use —
      Chorus. — This poor old horse!

Irish Song

Sung by Murray of Holden, Maine, who says it was written by a fellow named Nesbeth, and that it had a chorus in Irish, which was not safe to sing in some parts of Bangor. Picked up in 1914 by W. M. Hardy.

1   It's of a gay wedding,
       As you soon shall hear,
    Got up in good style,
       An' it ain't far from here.

2   It's Arthur De Laney
       Tamson to Killrye;
    He was the darlint,
       The dancing bug boy.

3   Three hundred gay fellows
       That day marched along,
    All with their great cudgels
       Both brave and strong.

4   You'll think them the locusts
       From the E-gyptian plains,
    And like the wild devils
       Let loose from their chains.

The Dark-Eyed Sailor

Taken down (without title) in 1914 by W. M. Hardy from the singing of Murray in Holden, Maine.

This fragment, which curiously illustrates the accidents of tradition, consists of *disjecta membra* of "Fair Phœbe and her Dark-Eyed Sailor," a song common in English broadsides and still orally current in England, Scotland, and America. See *Journal of the Folk-Song Society*, IV, 129 ff. (text, tunes, and references); Ashton, *Real Sailor-Songs*, 71; Greig, *Folk-Song of the North-East*, CXII; broadsides of Catnach, Forth, and others. For this country, see *Marsh's Selection, or, Singing for the Million* (New York, 1854), III, 69–71; *Singer's Journal*, I, 39; de Marsan (New York) broadside, List 3, No. 71; Wehman (New York) broadside, No. 406.

1 As a comely fair maiden
   Was taking the air
   One evening fair,

2 She met a sailor all on her way,
   And I paid attention,
   And I paid attention
   To hear what they would say.

3 He says, "Pretty fair maiden,
      Whilst roam alone,
   The day is far spent,
      The night's coming on."

4 She said, while tears rolled in her eye,
   "[It] is but my dark-eyed sailor,
   [It] is but my dark-eyed sailor,
   That's proving my downfall.

5   "His dark brown eyes,
       His curly hair,
     His flattering tongue
       Did my heart ensnare."

6   Gently was he now . . . like you
     To advise a maiden
     To advise a maiden
     To . . .

7   We travelled o'er the mountain tops,
     When the hills were clad with snow.

FAIR PHŒBE AND HER DARK–EYED SAILOR

I GIVE the complete song from a broadside printed by Forth, Pocklington, Yorkshire (No. 78).

1   It's of a comely young lady fair,
     Was walking out to take the air,
     She met with a sailor upon her way,
     So I paid attention to hear what they did say.

2   Said William — lady why roam alone?
     The night is coming, and day near gone,
     She said while tears from her eyes did fall,
     It's a dark-ey'd sailor that's proving my downfall.

3   It's two long years since he left the land,
     I took a gold ring from off my hand,
     We broke the token — here's part with me,
     And the other rolling at the bottom of the sea.

4　Said William drive him all from your mind,
　　Some other sailor as good you'll find,
　　Love turns aside, and soon cold does grow,
　　Like a winter's morning when lands are cloth'd with
　　　　snow.

5　These words did Phœbe's fond heart inflame,
　　She said on me you shall play no game,
　　She drew a dagger and then did cry,
　　For my dark-ey'd sailor, a maid I'll live and die.

6　His coal-black eye, and his curly hair,
　　And pleasing tongue did my heart ensnare,
　　Genteel he was but no rake like you
　　To advise a maiden to slight the jacket blue.

7　But still said Phœbe, I'll ne'er disdain,
　　A tarry sailor, but treat the same,
　　So drink his health — here's a piece of coin,
　　But my dark-ey'd sailor still claims this heart of
　　　　mine.

8　Then half the ring did young William show,
　　She seem'd distracted 'midst joy and woe,
　　Oh, welcome William, I've lands and gold,
　　For my dark-ey'd sailor, so manly, true, and bold.

9　Now in a village down by the sea,
　　They're joined in wedlock, and well agree,
　　All maids be true when your love's away,
　　For a cloudy morning oft brings a pleasant day.

The Jacket So Blue

This song and "Far, Far at Sea" are from a broadside of about 1835, apparently of English origin. There is a crude woodcut of a ship in one corner. It was sent the editor by a retired seaman in Searsport, Maine, 1916; and in turn given by the editor to the Library of the University of Maine in 1917.

1 In Liverpool town,
      In fair Lancashire,
   I lived in splendor,
      And free from love's care.

2 I rolled in riches,
      And sweethearts not a few,
   I'm wounded by a sailor
      And his jacket so blue.

3 There came a crew of sailors
      And so on you shall hear,
   From Scotland to Liverpool,
      Abroad for to steer.

4 There is one among them
      I wish I ne'er knew,
   He's a bonny sailor lad
      With his jacket so blue.

5 His cheeks like the roses,
      His eyes like the slows.
   He is handsome and proper
      He kills where he goes.

6   He is handsome and proper
      And comely to view,
   He's a bonny sailor lad,
      With his jacket so blue.

7   When I go to my bed,
      I cannot find rest,
   The thoughts of my true love
      Still run in my breast.

8   The thoughts of my true love
      Still run in my view,
   He's a bonny sailor lad,
      And his jacket so blue.

9   Early one morning
      I arose from my bed,
   I called on Sally,
      She was my waiting maid.

10   To dress me as fine
      As her two hands could do,
   I'll away to see my sailor
      With his jacket so blue.

11   She was instantly dress'd
      And the wharf did attend,
   She stood with impatience
      To hear her love nam'd.

12   Charles Stewart they call'd him,
      Indeed it was true,
   Once a prince of that name
      Wore a jacket of blue.

13 My love passed by me,
   To the boat straight away,
   I strove to speak to him
   But he could not stay.

14 I strove to speak to him
   But away then he flew,
   My heart did go with him
   And his jacket so blue.

15 She says, "My dear sailor,
   I'll buy your discharge,
   I'll free you from the sea
   And set you at large.

16 "I'll free you from the sea
   If you will be true,
   And you'll never wear a stain
   On your jacket so blue."

17 He says, "My dear lady,
   You'll buy my discharge,
   You'll free me from the sea
   And set me at large.

18 "For all your kind offers
   I am obliged to you,
   But I'll never wear a stain
   On my jacket of blue.

19 "I have a dear girl
   In my own country,
   I will never forsake her
   For her poverty.

20   "To the girl that I love,
    I'll always prove true,
For I'll never wear a stain
    On my jacket of blue."

21   I'll send for a limner,
    Without more delay,
To draw my love's portrait
    That I may it see.

22   I'll set it in my chamber,
    Keep it close to my view,
And will think on my sailor
    With his jacket so blue.

Far, Far at Sea

THIS song, which was in the repertory of the famous singer Charles
Incledon (1763–1826), is printed in the *British Melodist*, 2d edi-
tion (London [1819]), pp. 128–129; *The Melodist* (London, 1828),
II, 306; *Grigg's Southern and Western Songster* (Philadelphia,
1829; also 1832, 1836, 1839), pp. 296–297; *The Norwich Minstrel*,
edited by J. S. Wells (Norwich, 1831), p. 19 ("Susan's Dream");
Fairburn's Everlasting Songster, 4th ed., p. 132; as well as in
English broadsides. The music, by C. H. Florio, is given in *The
Vocal Companion*, edited by John Parry (London, 1837), pp. 68–
69.

1   'T was night, when the bell had struck twelve.
      And poor Susan was laid on her pillow,
    In her ear whisper'd some fleeting elf —
      "Your love now lies toss'd on a billow,
        Far, far at Sea."

2   All was dark, when she woke out of breath,
      Not an object her fears could discover;
    All was still as the silence of death,
      Save fancy, which painted her lover
        Far, far at Sea.

3   So she whisper'd a pray'r — clos'd her eyes;
      But the phantom still haunted her pillow;
    While in terror she echo'd his cries,
      As struggling he sunk in a billow,
        Far, far at Sea.

The Flying Cloud

This ballad is known in Maine (A) and Michigan (B). Mackenzie in *The Quest of the Ballad*, pp. 151–153, quotes eight stanzas of an inferior variant sung in Nova Scotia. That variant gives "Robert Anderson" as the culprit. The main events are the same as in A, with occasional different wording and a slightly different distribution of details in the stanzas, especially in the opening ones. Another variant (from Scotland) is "William Hollander," in Greig's *Folk-Song of the North-East*, CXVIII.

A

"THE FLYING CLOUD": *text furnished by a retired sea-captain of Searsport, Maine, as printed in a Boston newspaper about 1916, which "was indebted to 'S. H.' of Westminster" for "a true copy."*

1   My name is Edward Hollohan,
  As you shall understand,
 I belong in the county of Waterford
  In Erin's happy land.

2   When I was young and in my prime,
  Kind fortune on me smiled,
 My parents doted on me —
  I being their only child.

3   My father bound me to a trade
  In Waterford's own town,
 He bound me to a cooper there
  By the name of William Brown.

4   I served my master faithfully
        For eighteen months or more,
    When I shipped on board the Ocean Queen
        Bound to Bermuda shore.

5   When I arrived at Bermuda shore
        I met with Captain Moore,
    The commander of the Flying Cloud,
        Belonging to Trimore.

6   So kindly he requested me
        On a slaving voyage to go,
    To the burning sands of Africa,
        Where the sugar cane doth grow.

7   We all agreed, excepting five,
        And those we had to land,
    Two of them being Boston men
        And two from Newfoundland.

8   The other was an Irishman,
        Belonging to Trimore,
    Oh, I wish to God I had joined those men
        And returned with them on shore.

9   The Flying Cloud was as fine a ship
        As ever swam the seas.
    Or ever hoisted a main topsail
        Before a lively breeze.

10   I have oftentimes seen our gallant ship
        As the wind lay abaft her wheel,
    With the royal and the skysail set aloft,
        Sail nineteen by the reel.

11   Oh, the Flying Cloud was a Spanish ship
        Of five hundred tons or more,
     She would outsail any other ship
        I ever saw before.

12   Her sails were like the drifting snow,
        On them there was no stain,
     And eighteen brass nine-pounder guns
        She carried abaft her main.

13   We sailed away without delay
        Till we came to the African shore,
     And eighteen hundred of those poor slaves
        From their native isle sailed o'er.

14   For we marched them all along our decks
        And stored them down below,
     And eighteen inches for a man
        Was all that they could go.

15   The very next day we sailed away
        With our cargo of slaves,
     'T would have been much better for those poor
        slaves
        Had they been in their graves;

16   For the plague and fever came on board,
        Swept half of them away;
     We dragged the dead up on the decks
        And threw them in the sea.

17   We sailed away without delay
        Till we came to the Cuban shore.
     We sold them to a planter there
        To be slaves forevermore;

18   The rice and coffee fields to hoe
        Beneath the burning sun,
      To lead a long and wretched life
        Till their career was run.

19   And when our money it was all gone
        We put to sea again.
      Then Captain Moore he came on board
        And said to us his men:

20   "There is gold and silver to be had
        If with me you will remain:
      We will hoist aloft a pirate's flag
        And we'll scour the raging main."

21   We robbed and plundered many a ship
        On the Spanish Main,
      And many's the widow and orphan child
        In sorrow must remain,

22   For we made their crews to walk the plank
        And gave them a watery grave;
      For the saying of our captain was:
        "A dead man tells no tales."

23   At length to Newgate we were brought,
        Bound down in iron chain,
      For robbing and plundering merchant ships
        Down on the Spanish Main.

24   It was drinking and bad company
        That made this wretch of me,
      Now, let young men a warning take —
        And a curse to piracy!

B

"THE FLYING CLOUD," *printed by Tolman in* The Journal of American Folk-Lore, *XXXV, 370–372.* "*Obtained by Mr. Hoyt E. Cooper, Manilla, Io., from Mr. Frank Covell, at the time assistant keeper, Split Rock Light, Minn., and from Mr. Ole Fonsted, Beaver Bay, Minn. Mr. Covell learned his songs in the neighborhood of Fremont, Mich. In one reference Mr. Cooper gave Mr. Covell's residence as Beaver Bay, Minn.*"

1   My name is Edward Hallahan,
      As you shall understand;
   I belong to the county of Waterford,
      In Erin's happy land.
   When I was young and in my prime,
      Kind fortune on me smiled;
   My parents reared me tenderly,
      I being their only child.

2   My father bound me to a trade
      In Waterford's own town;
   He bound me to a cooper there
      By the name of William Brown.
   I served my master faithfully
      For eighteen months or more;
   When I sailed on board the "Ocean Queen,"
      Bound for Bermuda's shore.

3   When we arrived at Bermuda's shore,
      I met with Captain Moore,
   The commander of "The Flying Cloud"
      Belonging to Trimore;

So kindly he requested me
　　Along with him to go
To the burning coast of Africa,
　　Where the sugar-cane doth grow.

4　We all agreed excepting five,
　　　And these we had to land,
　　Two of them being Boston men,
　　　And two from Newfoundland;
　　The other was an Irishman
　　　Belonging to Trimore.
　　Oh, I wish to God I had joined those men,
　　　And staid with them on shore!

5　"The Flying Cloud" was as fine a boat
　　　As ever sailed the seas,
　　As ever hoisted a maintopsail
　　　Before a lively breeze;
　　I have ofttimes seen our gallant ship,
　　　As the wind lay abaft her wheel,
　　With the royal and skysail set aloft,
　　　Sail nineteen by the reel.

6　Oh, "The Flying Cloud" was a Spanish boat,
　　　Of five hundred tons or more;
　　She would outsail any other ship
　　　I ever saw before.
　　Her sails were like the drifting snow,
　　　On them there was no stain;
　　And eighteen brass nine-pounder guns
　　　She carried abaft her main.

7   We sailed away without delay,
      Till we came to the African shore;
    And eighteen hundred of those poor slaves
      From their native isle [?] sailed o'er;
    For we marched them all along our decks,
      And stored them down below;
    Scarce eighteen inches to a man
      Was all they had to go.

8   The very next day we sailed away
      With our cargo of slaves.
    'T would have been much better for those poor
      souls
      Had they been in their graves;
    For the plague and the fever came on board,
      Swept half of them away.
    We dragged the dead upon the decks,
      And threw them in the sea.

9   We sailed away without delay,
      Till we came to the Cuban shore;
    We sold them to a planter there,
      To be slaves forevermore;
    The rice and coffee fields to hoe
      Beneath the burning sun,
    To lead a long and wretched life,
      Till their career was run.

10   And when our money was all gone,
      We put to sea again.
    Then Captain Moore he came on deck,
      And said to us his men,

"There's gold and silver to be had,
    If with me you will remain;
We will hoist aloft a pirate's flag,
    And we'll scour the raging main."

11   We robbed and plundered many a ship
    Down on the Spanish Main;
And many's the widow and orphan child
    In sorrow must remain;
For we made them to walk our gang-plank,
    And gave them a watery grave;
For the saying of our master was,
    "A dead man tells no tales."

12   At length to Newgate we were brought,
    Bound down in iron chain,
For robbing and plundering merchant ships
    Down on the Spanish Main.
It was drinking and bad company
    That made this wretch of me.
Now let young men a warning take,
    And a curse to piracy!

HISTORICAL BALLADS AND SONGS

Lovewell's Fight, I

THIS famous American ballad gives a substantially correct account of the battle between Captain John Lovewell and the Indians at Pigwacket (Pequawket), now Fryeburg, Maine, in May, 1725. The earliest text known is that printed by Farmer and Moore in *Collections, Historical and Miscellaneous; and Monthly Literary Journal*, Concord, New Hampshire, February, 1824, III, 64–66, and entitled "Lovewell's Fight. Song." The editors remark: "The following Song was written about one hundred years since. . . . For many years, it was sung throughout a considerable portion of New-Hampshire and Massachusetts. . . . Through the kindness of a friend, to whom we are also indebted for a copy of the song, we are favored with some notices of Captain Lovewell's family. . . ." It is reprinted (not with minute accuracy) in E. E. Hale's *New England History in Ballads* (Boston, 1903), pp. 69–75; in G. C. Eggleston's *American War Ballads and Lyrics*, I, 14–17, and elsewhere. I have reproduced the song exactly as it stands in the *Collections*, our only authority for the text. It may forestall misapprehension to add that Eggleston is mistaken in stating (I, 13) that the song "has been preserved in Penhallow's 'History of the Wars of New England with the Eastern Indians,' 1726." Penhallow gives a good account of Lovewell's expedition (pp. 112–117), but he neither preserves this song nor in any way alludes to it; in fact, he says nothing about any song or poem on the subject. The error undoubtedly arose from the fact that the ballad (from the *Collections*) is appended (with an exact indication of source) to the Cincinnati *reprint* of Penhallow (1859), pp. 129–131.

The *New-England Courant* for May 31, 1725, contains the following advertisement: "Just Publish'd, and sold by J. Franklin in Union-Street, The Voluntier's March; being a full and true

Account of the bloody Fight which happen'd between Capt.
Lovewell's Company, and the Indians at Pigwoket. An excellent
new Song" (W. C. Ford, *Massachusetts Broadsides*, No. 523,
p. 73). No copy of this broadside is known. Very likely it con-
tained the ballad now before us.

On this ballad and the next (also on the Fight itself) see S. G.
Drake's edition of Church's *Indian Wars*, 1829, Appendix, pp.
330–335; Drake's *Book of the Indians*, 5th ed., 1837, Book III,
pp. 129–133; C. J. Fox, *History of the Old Township of Dunstable*,
1846, pp. 124–131; N. Bouton's edition of *The Original Account
of Capt. John Lovewell's "Great Fight"* by the Rev. Thomas
Symmes, 1861, pp. 38–46; F. Kidder, *The Expeditions of Capt.
John Lovewell*, 1865, pp. 115–119 (reprint, ed. by G. W. Chamberlain, 1909, pp. 94–98); Elias Nason, *History of the Town of
Dunstable*, 1877, pp. 51–54; Harriet Martineau, *Retrospect of
Western Travel*, New York, 1838, II, 82; Williamson, *Bibliography of the State of Maine*, I, 467–468; II, 545; G. W. Chamberlain, *Maine Historical Society Collections and Proceedings*,
2d Series, IX, 9–12; Palfrey, *History of New England*, IV (1875),
442, note 1; Parkman, *A Half-Century of Conflict*, I (1892),
247–261.

LOVEWELL'S FIGHT

SONG

1   Of worthy Captain LOVEWELL,
       I purpose now to sing,
    How valiantly he served
       his country and his King;
    He and his valiant soldiers,
       did range the woods full wide,
    And hardships they endured
       to quell the Indian's pride.

2   'T was nigh unto Pigwacket,
      on the eighth day of May,
  They spied a rebel Indian
      soon after break of day;
  He on a bank was walking,
      upon a neck of land,
  Which leads into a pond
      as we're made to understand.

3   Our men resolv'd to have him,
      and travell'd two miles round,
  Until they met the Indian,
      who boldly stood his ground;
  Then speaks up Captain Lovewell,
      "take you good heed," says he,
  "This rogue is to decoy us,
      I very plainly see.

4   "The Indians lie in ambush,
      in some place nigh at hand,
  "In order to surround us
      upon this neck of land;
  "Therefore we'll march in order,
      and each man leave his pack,
  "That we may briskly fight them
      when they make their attack."

5   They came unto this Indian,
      who did them thus defy,
  As soon as they came nigh him,
      two guns he did let fly,

Which wounded Captain LOVEWELL,
    and likewise one man more,
But when this rogue was running,
    they laid him in his gore.

6   Then having scalp'd the Indian,
       they went back to the spot,
    Where they had laid their packs down,
       but there they found them not,
    For the Indians having spy'd them,
       when they them down did lay,
    Did seize them for their plunder,
       and carry them away.

7   These rebels lay in ambush,
       this very place hard by,
    So that an English soldier
       did one of them espy,
    And cried out, "here's an Indian,"
       with that they started out,
    As fiercely as old lions,
       and hideously did shout.

8   With that our valiant English,
       all gave a loud huzza,
    To shew the rebel Indians
       they fear'd them not a straw:
    So now the fight began,
       and as fiercely as could be,
    The Indians ran up to them,
       but soon were forced to flee.

9   Thus spake up Captain LOVEWELL,
      when first the fight began
"Fight on my valiant heroes!
      you see they fall like rain."
For as we are inform'd,
      the Indians were so thick,
A man could scarcely fire a gun
      and not some of them hit.

10   Then did the rebels try their best
      our soldiers to surround,
But they could not accomplish it,
      because there was a pond,
To which our men retreated
      and covered all the rear,
The rogues were forc'd to flee them,
      altho' they skulked for fear.

11   Two logs there were behind them
      that close together lay,
Without being discovered,
      they could not get away;
Therefore our valiant English,
      they travell'd in a row,
And at a handsome distance
      as they were wont to go.

12   'T was ten o'clock in the morning,
      when first the fight begun,
And fiercely did continue
      until the setting sun;

Excepting that the Indians
    some hours before 't was night,
Drew off into the bushes
    and ceas'd a while to fight,

13   But soon again returned,
      in fierce and furious mood,
Shouting as in the morning,
    but yet not half so loud;
For as we are informed,
    so thick and fast they fell,
Scarce twenty of their number,
    at night did get home well.

14   And that our valiant English,
      till midnight there did stay,
To see whether the rebels
    would have another fray;
But they no more returning,
    they made off towards their home,
And brought away their wounded
    as far as they could come.

15   Of all our valiant English,
      there were but thirty-four,
And of the rebel Indians,
    there were about fourscore.
And sixteen of our English
    did safely home return,
The rest were kill'd and wounded,
    for which we all must mourn.

16 Our worthy Captain LOVEWELL
        among them there did die,
    They killed Lieut. ROBBINS,
        and wounded good young FRYE,
    Who was our English Chaplain;
        he many Indians slew,
    And some of them he scalp'd
        when bullets round him flew.

17 Young FULLAM too I'll mention,
        because he fought so well,
    Endeavouring to save a man,
        a sacrifice he fell;
    But yet our valiant Englishmen
        in fight were ne'er dismay'd,
    But still they kept their motion,
        and WYMAN's Captain made,

18 Who shot the old chief PAUGUS,
        which did the foe defeat,
    Then set his men in order,
        and brought off the retreat;
    And braving many dangers
        and hardships in the way,
    They safe arriv'd at Dunstable,
        the thirteenth day of May.

Lovewell's Fight, II

FIRST printed in Farmer and Moore's *Collections, Historical and Miscellaneous; and Monthly Literary Journal*, Concord, New Hampshire, March, 1824, III, 94–97, with the note, "For the Monthly Literary Journal." I reprint it exactly, letter for letter and point for point, merely adding numbers for the stanzas. The poem was anonymous, but was probably written by the Rev. Thomas Cogswell Upham (1799–1872), then the minister of Rochester, New Hampshire, afterwards Professor of Mental and Moral Philosophy at Bowdoin College (1825–1867). I have a text differing from the original in a few minute points of expression which was furnished by Mrs. F. H. Eckstorm. She states that the ballad was taught her by her father (born in 1838) when she was a child, and that he learned it from his father.

An acknowledged poem of Upham's on Lovewell's Fight (beginning "Ah! where are the soldiers that fought here of yore?") is printed by Farmer and Moore in their *Collections*, I, 35–36 (1822); by Drake in his edition of Church, 1829, Appendix, pp. 335–336; by Bouton in his edition of Symmes, 1861, pp. 47–48; by Kidder, *The Expeditions of Capt. John Lovewell*, 1865, pp. 122–123 (reprint, 1909, pp. 101–102); by Nason, *History of the Town of Dunstable*, 1877, pp. 54–55; and in the Cincinnati edition of Penhallow (1859), p. 136.

Still another copy of verses, "The Mournfull Elegy of Mr. Jona. Frye, 1725," was printed for the first time (as communicated by T. C. Frye, of Andover, Massachusetts) in the *New England Historical and Genealogical Register*, 1861, XV, 91, with the remark: "These lines, traditions say, were written when the news of his death reached Andover, by a young girl to whom he had engaged himself against the wishes of his parents; their objections were want of property and education. Her name is lost." But Samuel L. Knapp, who had a manuscript copy, and who analyzes the poem in his *Lectures on American Literature* (New York, 1829), p. 157, gives the name of the authoress as Susannah Rogers, and this appears to be correct (see Williamson's *Bibliography*, II, 375). The elegy is reprinted (not quite exactly) by Bouton, pp. 35-37, by Kidder, pp. 120-122 (ed. 1909, pp. 99-101), and (very imperfectly) by Bailey, *Historical Sketches of Andover*, 1880, pp. 191-193. It begins:—

> Assist ye muses help my quill,
> Whilest floods of tears does down distill,
> Not from mine eyes alone; but all
> That hears the sad, and doleful fall
> Of that young student, Mr. Frye,
> Who in his blooming youth did die.

See stanzas 20-27, below.

𝔏𝔬𝔳𝔢𝔴𝔢𝔩𝔩'𝔰 𝔉𝔦𝔤𝔥𝔱.

A BALLAD.

1 What time the noble LOVEWELL came,
     With fifty men from Dunstable,
   The cruel Pequa'tt tribe to tame,
     With arms and bloodshed terrible.

2 Then did the crimson streams, that flowed,
     Seem like the waters of the brook,
   That brightly shine, that loudly dash
     Far down the cliffs of Agiochook.

3 With Lovewell brave, John Harwood came;
     From wife and babes 't was hard to part,
   Young Harwood took her by the hand,
     And bound the weeper to his heart.

4   Repress that tear, my Mary, dear,
    Said Harwood to his loving wife,
It tries me hard to leave thee here,
    And seek in distant woods the strife.

5   When gone, my Mary, think of me,
    And pray to God, that I may be,
Such as one ought that lives for thee,
    And come at last in victory.

6   Thus left young Harwood babe and wife,
    With accent wild, she bade adieu;
It grieved those lovers much to part,
    So fond and fair, so kind and true.

7   Seth Wyman, who in Woburn lived,
    (A marksman he of courage true,)
Shot the first Indian, whom they saw,
    Sheer through his heart the bullet flew.

8   The Savage had been seeking game,
    Two guns and eke a knife he bore,
And two black ducks were in his hand,
    He shrieked, and fell, to rise no more.

9   Anon, there eighty Indians rose,
    Who'd hid themselves in ambush dread;
Their knives they shook, their guns they aimed,
    The famous Paugus at their head.

10   Good heavens! they dance the Powow dance,
    What horrid yells the forest fill?
The grim bear crouches in his den,
    The eagle seeks the distant hill.

11 What means this dance, this Powow dance?
    Stern Wyman said; with wondrous art,
He crept full near, his rifle aimed,
    And shot the leader through the heart.

12 John Lovewell, captain of the band,
    His sword he waved, that glittered bright,
For the last time he cheered his men,
    And led them onward to the fight.

13 Fight on, fight on, brave Lovewell said,
    Fight on, while heaven shall give you breath!
An Indian ball then pierced him through,
    And Lovewell closed his eyes in death.

14 John Harwood died all bathed in blood,
    When he had fought, till set of day;
And many more we may not name,
    Fell in the bloody battle fray.

15 When news did come to Harwood's wife,
    That he with Lovewell fought and died,
Far in the wilds had given his life,
    Nor more would in their home abide;

16 Such grief did seize upon her mind,
    Such sorrow filled her faithful breast;
On earth, she ne'er found peace again,
    But followed Harwood to his rest.

17 'T was Paugus led the Pequa'tt tribe; —
    As runs the Fox, would Paugus run;
As howls the wild wolf, would he howl,
    A large bear skin had Paugus on.

18   But Chamberlain, of Dunstable,
          (One whom a savage ne'er shall slay,)
      Met Paugus by the water side,
          And shot him dead upon that day.

19   Good heavens! Is this a time for pray'r?
          Is this a time to worship God?
      When Lovewell's men are dying fast,
          And Paugus' tribe hath felt the rod?

20   The Chaplain's name was Jonathan Frye;
          In Andover his father dwelt,
      And oft with Lovewell's men he'd prayed,
          Before the mortal wound he felt.

21   A man was he of comely form,
          Polished and brave, well learnt and kind;
      Old Harvard's learned halls he left,
          Far in the wilds a grave to find.

22   Ah! now his blood red arm he lifts,
          His closing lids he tries to raise;
      And speak once more before he dies,
          In supplication and in praise.

23   He prays kind heaven to grant success,
          Brave Lovewell's men to guide and bless,
      And when they've shed their heart blood true,
          To raise them all to happiness.

24   Come hither, Farwell, said young Frye,
          You see that I'm about to die;
      Now for the love I bear to you,
          When cold in death my bones shall lie;

25 Go thou and see my parents dear,
      And tell them you stood by me here;
    Console them when they cry, Alas!
      And wipe away the falling tear.

26 Lieutenant Farwell took his hand,
      His arm around his neck he threw,
    And said, brave Chaplain, I could wish,
      That heaven had made me die for you.

27 The Chaplain on kind Farwell's breast,
      Bloody and languishing he fell;
    Nor after this said more, but *this*,
      "I love thee, soldier, fare thee well."

28 Ah! many a wife shall rend her hair,
      And many a child cry, "Woe is me!"
    When messengers the news shall bear,
      Of Lovewell's dear bought victory.

29 With footsteps slow shall travellers go,
      Where Lovewell's pond shines clear and bright,
    And mark the place, where those are laid,
      Who fell in Lovewell's bloody fight.

30 Old men shall shake their heads, and say,
      Sad was the hour and terrible,
    When Lovewell brave 'gainst Paugus went,
      With fifty men from Dunstable.

Beside the Kennebec

PRINTED in the *New York Journal of Commerce*. It was found in a scrap-book, made about 1861, in the Harris Collection, John Hay Library, Brown University. This song, obviously modern, refers to Benedict Arnold's Expedition against Quebec in the autumn of 1775.

1   They marched with Arnold at their head,
      Our soldiers true and brave,
    To far off heights of Canada,
      By wood and rock and wave.

2   They left the scenes behind, perchance
      They might not see again;
    The homesteads fair, the fields which smiled
      With autumn's ripened grain.

3   And forth they marched to meet the foe,
      The invader's course to check,
    When the autumn leaves were brightening
      Along the Kennebec.

4   On through the deep and darkening wood,
      Through bush and brake and brier,
    The wolf howl round their path by day,
      By night beyond their fire, —

5   Their camp-fire, where all travel-worn,
      When fording lake and stream,
    Chilled with the wave, with hunger faint,
      They laid them down to dream

6   Of those dear homes they left behind;
       A dim and lessening speck,
    When they marched away to Canada,
       Beside the Kennebec.

7   And one a brave and noble boy,
       With kindling cheek and eye,
    Whose smile and voice brought light to all,
       Lay down at last to die:

8   To die of hunger's gnawing pain,
       A fate that some must share,
    Who closed with tears his soft blue eyes,
       And heard his dying prayer.

9   They took a bright curl from his brow, —
       The 'kerchief from his neck,
    And laid him neath the autumn leaves,
       Beside the Kennebec.

10   Within a fair New England home,
       Are kept those relics yet;
    The story of our Stormy Past
       True hearts will not forget.

11   A sister's son kept bright this theme,
       It passed from son to son: —
    And now when winter evenings come
       And talk and song are done,

12   The grandsire tells the story o'er,
       With a tear he will not check,
    Of the boy who died so long ago,
       Beside the Kennebec.

The Squatters of Maine

From the *Independent Chronicle* (Boston), May 19, 1806, where it is marked "For the Chronicle." Printed also as a broadside soon after (Isaiah Thomas's collection, made in 1813, I, 18, American Antiquarian Society).

The occasion for this lively political song was the Massachusetts election of 1806, when the District of Maine was still a part of that state. In Massachusetts proper ("old Massachusetts") the Federalists were in the majority, but Maine was Democratic or Republican (then synonymous terms). The vote was uncomfortably close for the Federalists, and the returns from Maine, which came in slowly, suggested a Democratic victory. It was thought that, if there proved to be no choice by the people, the Democrats (reinforced by the members from Maine) would carry the day in the General Court. On April 30 the *Columbian Centinel* (Federalist) indulged editorially in a petulant outburst: "The question now is, shall the *squatters* of *Maine* impose a Governor on *Massachusetts?*" Next day the Boston *Independent Chronicle* (Democratic) quoted this sentence, remarking "This is the gentlemanly language of the Centinel of Yesterday. It evinces the true spirit of federalism," etc. In the same number the *Chronicle* rings the changes, with elaborate irony, on the word *squatters*. The song, it will be observed, was composed by some Democrat in the same ironical vein. It purports to be an exhortation to the Federalists to defend "old Massachusetts" against the wicked Maine squatters in the legislature. For historical details see Stanwood's paper on *The Massachusetts Election of 1806* (*Massachusetts Historical Society Proceedings*, 2d Series, XX, 12–19).

"THE SQUATTERS OF MAINE"

A New Song

1   Approach ye *Feds*, in phalanx brave,
     With mien and visage ireful;
     Our own and *Britain's* cause to save —
     Prepare for battle direful.

CHORUS
For Maine her "squatters" sends to town,
On legislative station;
The "Boston host" to batter down,
Those guardians of the nation.

2   Where *Massasoit* and *Philip* rul'd,
       And *Strong* of later date sirs;
    Shall we, by *eastern sachems* school'd,
       Lose all our power in state sirs?

CHORUS
When Maine &c.

3   No: join as one, with heart and hand,
       "Exterminate" this faction,
    And save this hapless sinking land,
       By such a *noble action.*

CHORUS
When Maine &c.

4   Then we again possess'd of power,
       Our former arts will practise;
    Each *democrat* shall rue the hour,
       When first he dare detract us.

CHORUS
When Maine &c.

5   Each *noble* and *ignoble Fed,*
       And *Feds* of each gradation;
    And all, who fed'ral vengeance dread,
       Attend this exhortation.

CHORUS
When Maine &c.

The Constitution and the Guerriere

THIS song was published in the *Boston Gazette* of September 7, 1812, and the *Columbian Centinel* of September 9, with the title "Ode." The capture of the Guerriere by the Constitution, under the command of Captain Isaac Hull, took place on August 19, 1812. There was a public dinner to Hull in Faneuil Hall on September 5, for which this poem was written by Lucius Manlius Sargent (1786–1867), later celebrated for his *Temperance Tales.* The *Boston Gazette* reports that "after the 5th Toast, the following original Ode was sung by Mr. Stebbins, with his usual taste and elegance, and was received with great applause." The Ode may be found also in other newspapers of the time — for example, in *The Weekly Messenger* (Boston), September 11, 1812; in the *Salem Gazette*, September 11; and in the *Franklin Herald* (Greenfield, Massachusetts), September 22. In 1814 it was included in *The Columbian Harmonist* (New York), pp. 134–136, and in 1815 in *The Songster's Companion* (Brattleborough, Vermont), pp. 297–299.

The text given below follows the *Gazette* in every particular, except that the stanzas have been numbered, the lines indented, and two misprints corrected in stanza 3: *bell'wring* (line 8) and *thunder's* (line 10). The Ode is less accurately reprinted by McCarty, *Songs, Odes, and Other Poems on National Subjects* (Philadelphia, 1842), II, 216–218; by G. C. Eggleston, *American War Ballads and Lyrics*, I, 128–130; by Admiral Luce, *Naval Songs*, 2d ed., 1902, pp. 28–29; and by B. E. Stevenson, *Poems of American History*, p. 296.

A copy sent to the editor by a retired seaman in Searsport, Maine, in 1916, shows no variant readings of importance, except *volleys* instead of *volumes* in stanza 3. Luce reads *vollies*.

ODE,

*Sung at the Dinner, given to the Officers of the
United States Frigate* Constitution, *after the
Victory over the British Frigate* Guerriere.

BY L. M. SARGENT, ESQ.

TUNE — *"Ye Mariners of England."*

1   BRITANNIA's gallant streamers
      Float proudly o'er the tide;
    And fairly wave Columbia's stripes,
      In battle, side by side.
    And ne'er did bolder foemen meet,
      Where ocean's surges pour.
    O'er the tide now they ride,
      While the bell'wing thunders roar,
        While the cannon's fire is flashing fast,
        And the bell'wing thunders roar.

2   When Yankee meets the Briton,
      Whose blood congenial flows,
    By Heav'n created to be friends,
      By fortune render'd foes;
    Hard then must be the battle fray,
      Ere well the fight is o'er.
    Now they ride, side by side,
      While the bell'wing thunders roar,
        While the cannon's fire is flashing fast,
        And the bell'wing thunders roar.

3   Still, still for noble England,
      Bold DACRES' streamers fly;
And, for Columbia, gallant HULL's,
     As proudly and as high.
Now louder rings the battle din,
     More thick the volumes pour;
Still they ride, side by side,
     While the bell'wing thunders roar,
      While the cannon's fire is flashing fast,
     And the bell'wing thunders roar.

4   Why lulls Britannia's thunder,
      That wak'd the wat'ry war?
Why stays that gallant Guerriere,
     Whose streamer wav'd so fair?
That streamer drinks the ocean wave!
     That warrior's fight is o'er!
Still they ride, side by side,
     While Columbia's thunders roar,
      While her cannon's fire is flashing fast,
     And her Yankee thunders roar.

5   Hark! 'tis the Briton's lee gun!
      Ne'er bolder warrior kneel'd!
And ne'er to gallant mariners
     Did braver seamen yield.
Proud be the sires, whose hardy boys,
     Then fell, to fight no more;
With the brave, mid the wave,
     When the cannon's thunders roar,
      Their spirits then shall trim the blast,
     And swell the thunder's roar.

6   Vain were the cheers of Britons,
        Their hearts did vainly swell,
     Where virtue, skill, and bravery,
        With gallant MORRIS fell.
     That heart, so well in battle tri'd,
        Along the Moorish shore,
     Again o'er the main,
        When Columbia's thunders roar,
           Shall prove its Yankee spirit true,
           When Columbia's thunders roar.

7   Hence be our floating bulwarks
        Those oaks our mountains yield;
     'Tis mighty Heaven's plain decree —
        Then take the wat'ry field!
     To ocean's farthest barrier then
        Your whit'ning sail shall pour;
     Safe they'll ride o'er the tide,
        While Columbia's thunders roar,
           While her cannon's fire is flashing fast,
           And her Yankee thunders roar.

Enterprise and Boxer

PRINTED in *The Bird of Birds*, 1818. This ballad celebrates the
capture of the British brig *Boxer* (Captain Samuel Blyth) by
the American brig *Enterprise*, under the command of Lieutenant
William Burrows, on September 5, 1813. Early in the engagement Blyth was killed and Burrows mortally wounded. The
Boxer was brought as a prize into Portland harbor. "No incident
in this quasi-civil war touched the sensibilities of the people more
deeply than the common funeral of the two commanders, — both
well known and favorites in the service, buried, with the same
honors and mourners, in the graveyard at Portland overlooking
the scene of the battle" (Henry Adams, *History of the United
States*, VII, 283). The order of the funeral procession may be
found in the *Columbian Centinel* (Boston) of September 11, 1813.
The same issue contains an account of the fight, extracted from
the Portland *Argus*.

Another contemporary American song (McCarty, II, 58) on
the same sea-fight pays a tribute to both commanders:

> The victory gain'd, we count the cost,
> We mourn, indeed, a hero lost!
>   Who nobly fell, we know, sirs;
> But Burrows, we with Lawrence find,
> Has left a living name behind,
>   Much honour'd by the foe, sirs.
>
> And while we notice deeds of fame,
> In which the gallant honours claim,
>   As heroes of our story,
> The name of Blyth a meed demands,
> Whose tomb is deck'd by foemen's hands,
>   Who well deserve the glory.

1   Come all ye sons of Freedom,
       Come, listen unto me,
     I'll relate to you an engagement
       Which happened on the sea,

2   Between the *Enterprise* and *Boxer*,
       Two noble ships of fame,
     Though the *Enterprise* is but small
       Soon made the *Boxer* tame.

3   It was off Portland harbor
       We cruised for a space,
     When meeting a British sloop of war,
       To them we showed our face.

4   We sent to them a challenge,
       Wishing for them to see.
     But they refused to accept of it
       And face their enemies.

5   All on third of September,
       It being a glorious day,
     We fell in with the *Boxer*,
       And had a bloody fray.

6   It being about *Meridian*
       When we to them drew near,
     We up with *Yankee Colors*,
       And gave to them three cheers.

7   As we were sailing near that harbor,
       With a sweet and pleasant gale,
     The saucy *Boxer* hovering round,
       And proudly spread her sail.

8   Until the *Enterprise* box'd her,
       And quickly made them see
    That we *all* were *Yankee heroes*
       Just from America.

9   So now we've gain'd the VICTORY,
       My Yankee hearts of steel,
    Let's save our enemies lives,
       Who now to us must yield.

10   When we came on board my boys,
       'T would grieve your hearts full sore,
    To see those proud Englishmen
       Lay bleeding in their gore.

11   Come now our fight is ended,
       And we'll go home with speed,
    To join those Americans
       Who've done such warlike deeds.

12   Then we'll join in choruses,
       And this shall be our song,
    "Good luck attend *our Navy*
       In hopes 'twill flourish long."

13   It's now in Portland harbor
       Our lucky ship does lay,
    May God bless Lieutenant *Burrows*,
       And all his warlike band.

14   Now we'll go on shore my boys,
       Where Liberty does dwell,
    It's one of the greatest blessings,
       That nothing can excel.

You Parliament of England

ADMIRAL LUCE, who prints a very imperfect text of this song (with tune) in his *Naval Songs*, 2d ed. (New York, 1902), p. 57, makes the following interesting note (p. viii): "'Ye Parliament of England,' was published, from an old Mss. copy, in the Portland, Me., *Advertiser*, in 1880, coupled with the request that anyone knowing the air, would kindly furnish it. For the *Enterprise* brought her prize, the *Boxer*, into Portland (a fact recorded in the fifth stanza), where the song was for years very popular. The request was complied with by Mr. Z. Thompson, who, under date of November 15th, 1880, wrote that he had sung the song when a boy, more than sixty years ago, and could still sing it. The air, as now published, was taken down from his rendering." The present editor has not found the song in oral circulation in Maine. Oddly enough, however, Miss Pound has recovered a fragment of it in Nebraska. She quotes four lines (stanza 5), but seems not to have identified the piece (*Folk-Song of Nebraska and the Central West*, p. 69; *Poetic Origins and the Ballad*, pp. 203–204).

The date of the song may be rather accurately fixed as between the latter part of September, 1813 (when Perry's Victory of September 10 became known: stanza 6), and the end of the year (for the *Essex* reached Portsmouth on December 13, 1813, on her return from her cruise: see stanza 11).

The text here printed follows that in *The American Songster*, edited by John Kenedy, Baltimore, 1836, pp. 214–217. The text in McCarty, *Songs, Odes*, etc., 1842, II, 76–79, is practically identical. After the close of the War of 1812, the song was revised to fit new conditions. In this later form it may be found in various "songsters," — for example, in *The Forget Me Not Songster* (Philadelphia and New York, Turner & Fisher), pp. 87–89. Stanza 9 is omitted. Stanza 11 (which follows 8) will be found on the next page.

Our Decatur in the Guerriere,
    Soon humbled the Turkish crew;
Bro't them to submission,
    As he has done to you.
The Essex in the South seas,
    Had put out all your lights;
The flag she wore at her mast's head,
    Was "free trade and sailor's rights."

Then follows stanza 10 ("Grant us free trade," etc.), which concludes the song. The adaptation must have been made after Decatur's exploits of June, 1815.

1   You parliament of England,
      you *lords* and *commons*, too,
    Consider well what you're about,
      and what you mean to do;
    You're now at war with Yankees —
      I'm sure you'll rue the day,
    You roused the sons of liberty,
      in North America.

2   You first confin'd our commerce,
      you said our ships shan't trade,
    You then impress'd our seamen,
      and us'd them as your slaves,
    You then insulted Ro[d]gers,
      while cruising on the main,
    And had we not declared war,
      you'd done it o'er again.

3   You thought our frigates were but few,
      and Yankees could not fight,
    Until bold Hull the Guerriere took,
      and banish'd her from sight;

The Wasp next took your Frolic,
    you nothing said to that,
The Poictiers being off the coast,
    of course you took her back.

4   Next, your Macedonian,
        no finer ship could swim,
    Decatur took her *gilt work* off,
        and then he took her in;
    The Java by a Yankee ship
        was sunk, you all must know,
    The Peacock fine, in all her pride,
        by Lawrence down did go.

5   Then you sent your Boxer,
        to beat us all about,
    But we had an *Enterprising* brig,
        that beat the Boxer out;
    Then *box'd* her up to Portland,
        and moor'd her off the town,
    To show the sons of liberty,
        the Boxer of renown.

6   Then upon lake Erie,
        brave Perry had some fun,
    You own he beat your naval force,
        and caused them to run;
    While Chauncey on Ontario,
        the like ne'er known before,
    A British squadron beat complete;
        some took, some ran ashore.

7   Then your "*Brave Indian Allies*,"
       you styl'd them by that name,
    Until they turn'd the tomahawk,
       then "*Savages*," became;
    Your mean insinuations
       they despised from their souls,
    And join'd the sons of liberty,
       that scorn'd to be controll'd.

8   Now remember, you Briton,
       far distant is the day,
    That all you gain'd by British force,
       you lost in America;[1]
    Go tell your king and parliament,
       by all the world its known,
    That British force by sea and land
       by Yankees is o'erthrown.

9   Use ev'ry endeavour
       to try to cause a peace,
    For Yankee ships are building fast,
       their navy to increase;
    They will enforce their commerce;
       their laws by Heaven were made,
    That Yankee ships, in time of peace,
       to any port might trade.

---

[1] "That all you'll gain by British force, you lost America" (Broadside in Harvard College Library). "That e'er you'll gain by British force your lost America" (McCarty).

10   Grant us free trade and commerce;
         don't impress our men,
      Give up all claims to Canada,
         then we'll make peace again;
      Then, England, we'll respect you,
         and treat you as a friend;
      Respect our flag and citizens,
         then all these wars will end.

11   Our Ro[d]gers, in the President,
         will burn, sink, and destroy,
      The Congress on the Brazil coast
         your commerce will annoy,
      The Essex on the South Sea,
         will put out all your lights,
      The flag she wears at her mast head,
         "Free Trade and Sailors' Rights!!!"

The Aroostook War

THIS song, and the two that follow, relate to the so-called Aroostook War in 1839. The dispute as to the boundary between Maine and New Brunswick led to aggressive acts on both sides. Rufus McIntire, the Maine land agent, was seized by armed New Brunswickers in the night of February 12, 1839, and taken to Fredericton jail. On the 13th, Sir John Harvey, Lieutenant Governor of New Brunswick, issued a proclamation stating that the province had been invaded and calling for a draft of soldiers. This was regarded as a declaration of war, and within a week a large number of Maine men had taken up arms, acting under orders from Governor Fairfield. On the 17th, McLaughlin, warden of the public lands in New Brunswick, and Captain Tibbets of the Tobique settlement, were brought as prisoners to Bangor. Negotiations, however, led to the withdrawal of the Maine troops in March and April, and no blood was shed. The question was settled by the Webster-Ashburton Treaty of 1842. See J. F. Sprague, *Historical Collections of Piscataquis County, Maine* (Dover, 1910), I, 216 ff.; *Aroostook War. Historical Sketch and Roster of Commissioned Officers and Enlisted Men* (Augusta, 1904).

These verses were found among the papers of the late Colonel Charles Jarvis of Ellsworth, Maine, who, in 1839, was appointed by Governor Fairfield to take charge of affairs on the Aroostook River after McIntire had been kidnapped. One of the men wrote these lines while sitting by the campfire one winter night. These facts are supplied by Mary A. Greely of Ellsworth, 1916.

1   Ye soldiers of Maine,
      Your bright weapons prepare:
   On your frontier's arising
    The clouds of grim war.

2   Your country's invaded,
      Invaded the soil
  Which your fathers have purchased
      With life-blood and toil.

3   Then "Hail the British!"
      Does any one cry?
  "Move not the old landmarks,"
      The settlers reply.

4   "Move not the old landmarks,"
      The scriptures enjoin,
  For our sons of Columbia
      Are west of the line.

The Soldiers' Song

As printed (with the date "Bangor, Feb. 21, 1839") in *Historical Collections of Piscataquis County* (Dover, 1910), I, 320–321. It is there credited to "Maine Newspapers, 1839."

TUNE — *Auld Lang Syne*

1   We are marching on to Madawask,
        To fight the trespassers;
     We'll teach the British how to walk —
        And come off conquerors.

2   We'll have our land right good and clear,
        For all the English say;
     They shall not cut another log,
        Nor stay another day.

3   They need not think to have our land,
        We Yankees can fight well;
     We've whipped them twice most manfully,
        As every child can tell.

4   And if the Tyrants say one word,
        A third time we will show,
     How high the Yankee spirit runs,
        And what our guns can do.

5   They better much all stay at home,
        And mind their business there;
     The way we treated them before,
        Made all the Nations stare.

6   Come on! brave [1] fellows, one and all!
      The Red-coats ne'er shall say,
    The Yankees feared to meet them armed,
      So gave our land away.

7   We'll feed them well with ball and shot.
      We'll cut these Red-coats down,
    Before we yield to them an inch
      Or title of our ground.

8   Ye Husbands, Fathers, Brothers, Sons,
      From every quarter come!
    March, to the bugle and the fife!
      March, to the beating drum!

9   Onward! my Lads so brave and true
      Our Country's right demands
    With justice, and with glory fight,
      For these Aroostook lands.

[1] Misprinted *brace*.

Maine Battle Song

ANOTHER contemporary song of the Aroostook War. Printed, without explanation, by McCarty, *Songs, Odes, and Other Poems on National Subjects*, 1842, III, 437–438. It appeared in Maine newspapers in 1839 (*Historical Collections of Piscataquis County, Maine*, Dover, 1910, I, 321).

1   Come, sogers! take your muskets up;
      And grasp your faithful rifles;
    We're gwoin to lick the red coat men,
      Who call us Yankees, "trifles."
    Bring out the big gun made of brass,
      Which forges July thunder;
    Bring out the flag of Bennington,
      And strike the foe with wonder.

2   We'll lick the red coats, any how,
      And drive them from the border;
    The loggers are awake — and all
      Await the gin'ral's order;
    Britannia shall not rule the Maine,
      Nor shall she rule the water,
    They've sung that song full long enough,
      Much longer than they oughter.

3   The Aroostook's a right slick stream,
      Has nation sights of woodlands,
    And hang the feller that would lose
      His footing on such good lands.

And all along the boundary line,
   There's pasturing for cattle;
But where that line of boundary is,
   We must decide by battle.

4   We do not care about the land,
     But they shan't hook it from us;
  Our country, right or wrong, we cry —
     No budging or compromise.
  So — beat the sheepskin — blow the fife,
     And march in training order;
  Our way is through the wilderness,
     And all along the border.

The Cumberland Crew

THE United States frigate Cumberland, commanded by Lieutenant George Morris, was sunk by the Merrimac off Newport News, Virginia, on March 8, 1862 (see Spears, *History of Our Navy*, 1897, IV, 197–207). I print this song as it was sung to me in 1916 by Mr. Fowler of Mattawamkeag, Maine, and taken down by his grandson. It differs slightly from the printed texts, which, however, are by no means identical in phraseology. Some of the variant readings are given in the footnotes (from Hayward).

See J. Henry Hayward, *Poetical Pen-Pictures of the War*, 3d ed. (New York, 1864), pp. 233–234 (title, "Monitor and Merrimac"; signature, "One of the Crew"); Lieder's *New York One-Cent Ballad Sheet*, Vol. I, No. 2, p. 15; *Partridge's New National Songster*, Vol. I, No. 1; *Adventure* (magazine) for August 20, 1922, p. 191; Luce, *Naval Songs*, 2d ed. (New York, 1902), pp. 138–139. Henry de Marsan, New York, printed the song as a broadside (List 19, No. 12), but I have not succeeded in finding this.

1   Oh comrades, come listen, and join in my ditty [1]
    Of a terrible battle that happened of late.
    May each Union tar shed a sad tear of pity
        When they think of the once gallant Cumberland's fate.
    For the eighth day of March [2] told a terrible story:
        The most of our seamen to the swells made acclaim; [3]
    Our flag it was wrapt in a mantle of glory
        By the heroic deeds of the Cumberland crew.

[1] "Oh comrades, come gather and join in my ditty" (Hayward).
[2] "On the 9th day of March told a terrible story."
[3] "And many a brave tar to this world bid adieu."

2   On the eighth day of March, about ten in the
  morning,
 The sky it was cloudless and bright shone the sun,
When the drum on the Cumberland sounded the
  warning
 Which told every seaman to stand by his gun;
When an ironclad came bearing down on us,
 And high in the air she the rebel flag flew;
The pennon of treason so proudly was waving
 Determined to conquer the Cumberland crew.

3   Then up steps our captain with firm resolution,
 Saying, "Boys, by this monster we'll ne'er be
  dismayed;
Let us fight for the Union's beloved constitution,
 To die for the Union we are not afraid.
Let us fight for the Union's own cause, it is glorious;
 For the stars and the stripes we will always prove
  true.
Let us die at our quarters or conquer victorious."
 He was answered with cheers from the Cumber-
  land crew.

4   Then our port we threw open and our guns we let
  thunder;
 Broadsides on the enemy like hail we did pour;
Our seamen they stood wrapt in great wonder,[1]
 When a shot struck her side and glanced harm-
  lessly o'er.

[1] "The people gazed, and struck with terror and wonder."

The pride of our navy could never be daunted.
 The dead and the dying our decks they did strew;
And the star-spangled banner stained
 By the blood of the Cumberland crew.[1]

5 When traitors found cannon no longer avail them
  For fighting those heroes with God on their side;
 The cause of secession no power to quail them,[2]
  The blood of our seamen it crimsoned the tide.
 She struck amidship, our plank she did sliver;
  Her sharp iron prow pierced our noble ship
   through;
 And as we were sinking in the dark rolling river,
  "We'll die at our guns," said the Cumberland
   crew.

6 Slowly she sunk in Virginia's dark waters;
  Our voices on the swells shall ne'er be heard more.[3]
 May be wept by Cumberland's brave sons and proud
   daughters![4]
 May our blood be avenged on Virginia's shore!
 In the battle-stained river so silently sleeping,
  And most of our voices to the swells bade adieu;[5]
 And the star-spangled banner so proudly was waving,
  Was nailed to the mast of the Cumberland crew.

[1] "The Flag of our Union; it boldly was planted,
 Sustained by the blood of the Cumberland's crew."
[2] "The power of Secessia had no power to quail them."
[3] "Their voices on earth will never be heard more."
[4] "They will be wept for by Columbia's sons and daughters."
[5] "And their souls have forever to this world bid adieu."

7   Columbia is the gem of the brightest communion.
      No flag ever floated so proudly before,
Now while those heroes who fought for the Union
      Beneath those bright stars so exultingly soar.[1]
When any brave heroes in battle assembled,
      God bless that dear banner, the red, white, and
        blue!
For beneath its bright fold we'll cause tyrants to
      tremble,
      Or die at our guns like the Cumberland crew.

[1] "For the spirit of those who died for the Union,
    Above its broad folds does exultingly soar."

Bay Billy

THIS spirited poem recounts an unusual incident in the history of
the 22d Maine at Fredericksburg. It was printed originally in
the *San Francisco News Letter* (now *Examiner*). The author is
Frank H. Gassaway. The text is from the authorized edition of
his *Poems*, 1920, pp. 38 ff., published by James T. White & Co.,
New York (to whom I am indebted for permission to print the
poem). It has long been a favorite of public reciters. In 1887
Mrs. Cora Urquhart Potter published through J. B. Lippincott
Co. *My Recitations*, in which "Bay Billy" is included, pp. 285 ff.
The preface is dated November 5th, 1886. It is found also in
various collections, as: Bates's *Cambridge Book of Poetry*; Pert-
wee's *Reciter's Treasury of Verse*; Shoemaker's *Best Selections*,
Vol. VIII; *Best Things from Best Authors*; *One Hundred Choice
Selections*, No. 20; Fobe's *Five Minute Recitations*; Shoemaker's
Practical Elocution; Anna Morgan's *Selected Readings*.

1   You may talk of horses of renown,
        What Goldsmith Maid has done,
    How Dexter cut the seconds down,
        And Fellowcraft's great run.
    Would you hear about a horse that once
        A mighty battle won?

2   'T was the last fight at Fredericksburg, —
        Perhaps the day you reck
    Our boys, the Twenty-second Maine,
        Kept Early's men in check.
    Just where Wade Hampton boomed away
        The fight went neck and neck.

3   All day we held the weaker wing,
       And held it with a will.
    Five several stubborn times we charged
       The battery on the hill.
    And five times beaten back, reformed,
       And kept our column still.

4   At last from out the centre fight
       Spurred up a general's aid,
    "That battery *must* silenced be!"
       He cried, as past he sped.
    Our colonel simply touched his cap,
       And then, with measured tread,

5   To lead the crouching line once more
       The grand old fellow came.
    No wounded man but raised his head
       And strove to gasp his name,
    And those who could not speak nor stir,
       "God blessed" him just the same.

6   For he was all the world to us,
       That hero gray and grim.
    Right well he knew that fearful slope
       We'd climb with none but him,
    Though while his white head led the way
       We'd charge hell's portals in.

7   This time we were not half-way up,
       When, 'midst the storm of shell,
    Our leader, with his sword upraised,
       Beneath our bay'nets fell,
    And, as we bore him back, the foe
       Set up a joyous yell.

8 Our hearts went with him. Back we swept,
  And when the bugle said,
 "Up, charge again!" no man was there
  But hung his dogged head.
 "We've no one left to lead us now,"
  The sullen soldiers said.

9 Just then before the laggard line
  The colonel's horse we spied,
 Bay Billy with his trappings on,
  His nostrils swelling wide,
 As though still on his gallant back
  The master sat astride.

10 Right royally he took the place
  That was of old his wont,
 And with a neigh that seemed to say,
  Above the battle's brunt,
 "How can the Twenty-second charge
  If *I* am not in front?"

11 Like statues rooted there we stood
  And gazed a little space,
 Above that floating mane we missed
  The dear familiar face,
 But we saw Bay Billy's eye of fire,
  And it gave us heart of grace.

12 No bugle call could rouse us all
  As that brave sight had done,
 Down all the battered line we felt
  A lightning impulse run.
 Up! up! the hill we followed Bill,
  And captured every gun!

13 And when upon the conquered height
   Died out the battle's hum,
Vainly 'mid living and dead
   We sought our leader dumb.
It seemed as if a spectre steed
   To win that day had come.

14 And then the dusk and dew of night
   Fell softly o'er the plain,
As though o'er man's dread work of death
   The angels wept again,
And drew night's curtain gently round
   A thousand beds of pain.

15 All night the surgeons' torches went
   The ghastly rows between —
All night with solemn step I paced
   The torn and bloody green.
But who that fought in the big war
   Such dread sights have not seen?

16 At last the morning broke. The lark
   Sang in the merry skies,
As if to e'en the sleepers there
   It bade, Wake, and arise!
Though naught but that last trump of all
   Could ope their heavy eyes.

17 And then once more, with banners gay,
   Stretched out the long brigade;
Trimly upon the furrowed field
   The troops stood on parade,
And bravely 'mid the ranks were closed
   The gaps the fight had made.

18   Not half the Twenty-second's men
       Were in their place that morn,
    And Corp'ral Dick, who yester-noon
       Stood six brave fellows on,
    Now touched my elbow in the ranks,
       For all between were gone.

19   Ah! who forgets that dreary hour
       When, as with misty eyes,
    To call the old familiar roll
       The solemn sergeant tries, —
    One feels that thumping of the heart
       As no prompt voice replies.

20   And as in falt'ring tone and slow
       The last few names were said,
    Across the field some missing horse
       Toiled up with weary tread,
    It caught the sergeant's eye, and, quick,
       Bay Billy's name he read.

21   Yes! there the old bay hero stood,
       All safe from battle's harms,
    And ere an order could be heard,
       Or the bugle's quick alarms,
    Down all the front from end to end
       The troops presented arms!

22   Not all the shoulder-straps on earth
       Could still our mighty cheer.
    And ever from that famous day,
       When rang the roll-call clear,
    Bay Billy's name was read, and then
       The whole line answered, "Here!"

MAINE BROADSIDES

When the Taters Are All Dug

THIS broadside was contributed by Mr. Chadburne of Mattawamkeag, Maine, in 1916. He bought it from a young fellow who had
finished work in the potato country and was without money. Mr.
Chadburne thinks him the author of it, but is not certain. The
young man thus paid his way.

"WHEN THE TATERS ARE ALL DUG"

[Tune of "Mother's Appeal to Her Boy"]

COMPOSED BY E. J. SULLIVAN

1 'Way up in Aroostook County
  Where in Winter falls the snow,
 Where in the short hot summer months
  The big potatoes grow;
 Where the farmers cuss and talk about
  Their big potato bugs,
 There's a smile all o'er the County,
  Till them 'taters are all dug.

2 In the village stores there's 'tater talk
  About their monstrous size;
 Some of these yarns they sound like truths,
  But a lot of them are lies;

There is no whiskey to be had,
  Spring water in a jug,
But there'll be an awful racket
  When them 'taters are all dug.

3   When the farmers start in digging
       They will stop you on your way,
     They will smoke and chew tobacco
       While they talk about the pay;
     They say, "fill up your baskets,
       Just as much as you can lug,"
     For they're always in a hurry
       Till them 'taters are all dug.

4   From East to West from North to South,
       The 'tater pickers came,
     Some had no cash for railroad fares,
       But they got there just the same;
     And how they sweat and cuss and pull
       And at the big potatoes tug,
     For the farmers have no use for them,
       When them 'taters are all dug.

5   And sometimes, too, a country girl
       Will pick up in the field,
     Some love-struck 'tater picker
       May cause her heart to yield;
     And in the evenings they'll beguile the time
       With a stolen kiss or hug;
     There is bound to be a wedding
       When the 'taters are all dug.

6   And when them 'taters are all dug
     And the pickers come to town,
     While the dollars in their pockets last,
     They never get a frown;
     Some of them go to the Line House,
     For to fill their little mug,
     'T is then they drop clean out of sight,
     For the 'taters are all dug.

The Bangor Fire

𝔇edicated to the 𝔓eople of 𝔅angor who 𝔏ost their 𝔥omes on 𝔖unday, 𝔄pril 30th, 1911

By JOHN J. FRIEND, BANGOR, MAINE

1   It was on a Sunday afternoon
        The sky was bright and clear,
    The people of our dear old town
        They felt no dread or fear;
    But 'ere the clock it had struck four
        They heard the signal bell
    Which drove them from the homes they loved
        And bid that last farewell.

2   Far down Broad Street the flames rose high,
        And crossed Kenduskeag Stream
    They landed at the Crosby shed,
        It seemed so like a dream;
    The savings bank is all afire
        Our Library is no more
    Oh! who would thought this Sabbath eve,
        Would bring sorrow to our door.

3   I'm standing on Exchange Street,
        To view this awful scene
    The Stearns block is toppling down,
        Great heavens what can it mean!
    And just across, the Morse-Oliver
        Is falling o'er our head
    And gazing there with anxious fear,
        Upon the aged dead.

4   Old Granite Block it has gone down,
       That landmark known to you
    The Universalist on the hill,
       That looked so bright and new;
    The First Baptist on Harlow Street
       The flames have entered there,
    Where but an hour or two before
       They knelt in silent prayer.

5   Please come with me to old Broadway,
       The First Church it s[t]ood there,
    'Twas built by Bangor's grand old stock,
       When life was young and fair;
    And that old bell with mellow tones
       'Twas cast by Paul Revere,
    It's silent now, it's heard no more
       We'll drop the heartfelt tear.

6   To French Street now I look again,
       The Third Church walls are bare,
    Home after home they have gone down,
       It fills us with despair;
    And old St. John's, that Gothic pile
       To memory ever dear,
    And that loved bell, whose grand deep tones,
       Was music to the ear.

7   I'm standing here on Somerset
       To view that sad, sad scene,
    On Centre, Spring and Cumberland,
       Our homes no more are seen;

And those grand elms whose shades we sought
   At the closing of the day,
Are mouldering into ashes
   As I sing my doleful lay.

8   Come back with me to Harlow Street,
     The High School it stood there,
Where early in the morning,
     The girls and boys so fair;
They came from every quarter
     And congregated here
There is naught but desolation
     On that spot we loved so dear.

9   Farewell unto the Windsor,
     And its walls that soared so high,
And also to the Graham Block,
     It was pleasing to the eye;
And dear old Norombega,
     Within whose walls, stood there
The artists, yes, from every land
     When life was young and fair.

10   To every one who gave his mite,
     Tho', much or little be,
Their names be written on the scroll,
     As they pass o'er life's dark sea;
And to our Mayor Mullen
     Who holds the leading reign,
May he stand for laws that true and just
     At Bangor down in Maine.

11   Now to our local firemen
          And strangers who came too,
      They fought as only men could fight,
          And showed their worth to you;
      And when the years have passed and gone,
          To children yet unborn
      They'll tell how they stood like pyramids
          To hail the coming morn.

12   There's one more verse it's to our God
          Who dwells beyond the skies,
      He can change our sad afflictions
          And let silver clouds roll by.
      For we'll clasp the hem of his garment
          Without a dread or fear,
      For in the hollow of his hand he holds us
          And can stay the silent tear.

President Wilson

Respectfully dedicated to our President, Woodrow Wilson,
our candidate for second term

By JOHN J. FRIEND, of BANGOR, MAINE

1   Come out Virginia's noble son
      We know that you are true,
The people of our grand old land
      They have their hope in you;
And with the power at our command
      We'll cast our vote again
To be chosen as our president,
      To hold the leading rein.

2   The people are the power you know
      Their acts should stand for right,
With Wilson as our leading star
      We'll win in this great fight;
There in that chair of state to rule,
      Where peace and plenty reign
And soldiers coming back once more
      To homes and friends again.

3   A modest unassuming man,
      A gentleman most true,
He's always stood for our just laws
      And proved his worth to you;
And when the years have passed and gone
      Sweet memories they'll recall,
Of what he's done for our good land
      To benefit us all.

4   And shall we win, our cause is just,
       The people's hope lies here,
     November's morning light appears,
       It's Wilson's name we hear.
     He's won the prize from hill and vale,
       They shout it o'er and o'er
     And with bowed heads to our great God,
       Whose name that we adore.

Bar Harbor By the Sea

𝔚𝔥𝔢𝔯𝔢 𝔜𝔬𝔲'𝔩𝔩 𝔐𝔢𝔢𝔱 𝔗𝔬𝔲𝔯𝔦𝔰𝔱𝔰 𝔬𝔣 𝔈𝔳𝔢𝔯𝔶 𝔏𝔞𝔫𝔡

By JOHN J. FRIEND, BANGOR, MAINE

1   The day was drawing to its close,
    · The sea was calm, the storm was o'er.
The pleasure yachts they sought repose,
    And stretched along from shore to shore;
And as I gazed upon that scene,
    And saw God's mighty works that day,
The sunlight cast its golden beams,
    On those grand hills far o'er the bay.

2   Bar Harbor, how I love thy hills,
    And valleys too so dear to me,
Where first I saw the light of day
    In that little village by the sea;
And when at eve I sought repose,
    Down by that shore so dear to me,
I watched the moon rise in the east,
    And cast its bright light o'er the sea.

3   And looking at Green Mountain there,
    In silent majesty arose,
To meet again the friends we love
    Who come once more to seek repose;
Here to regain their wasted strength
    And rest that tired, weary brain,
I'm speaking of an Island now,
    Bar Harbor, down in dear old Maine.

4   Of Miss Belle Gurnee now I speak,
     She is a little queen,
   She labored hard for the soldiers,
     As everyone has seen;
   And to those noble women,
     Who gave their time, its true,
   May God's blessing follow each one of them
     For they are the real true blue.

5   True friends will meet the Livingstons
     In their cottages of ease,
   And the Endicotts whom we welcome here
     In their cottage by the sea;
   And also Ketterlinus
     From Philadelphia, he's come down,
   To meet true friends and neighbors,
     In old Bar Harbor town,

6   Its here you'll meet the Harrisons,
     In their cottages so fair,
   And the Morgans whom we welcome here,
     To enjoy the summer air;
   And hundreds of the good old stock,
     You'll meet in grand array
   To watch the ocean's waves that roll
     And while the hour away.

7   Of the Bar Harbor House now I speak
     Where the visitors may stay,
   To pass a week of leisure,
     And while the hours away;

To watch the ocean waves that roll,
   Against that rock bound shore,
And meet his genial proprietor
   Our honored, E. S. Moore.

8   Of William Fenley now I speak
        In life was just and true,
     With Freeman Higgins whose youth was spent
        In pleasant hours with you;
     And Capt. Frank Connor, that man of worth
        Who labored hard each day,
     There watched his pleasure yachts glide o'er
        The waves in Frenchman's bay.

9   I wish to speak of Mrs. May
        A noble name it's true,
     And Mrs. Montgomery Sears,
        Who's also known to you;
     She has always stood for the soldier's needs
        From Boston she's come down
     To meet true friends who honor her,
        In old Bar Harbor town.

10   And now I'll pass up to the right,
        There standing Mooseley Hall,
     The home of Howard in this life,
        Whose name was known to all;
     And as I gaze upon that scene,
        Of memories ever dear,
     I think of loved ones gone before
        And drop the silent tear.

11   Bar Harbor feels a pride dear friends,
       In the Redeemer's church it's true,
    Where rich and poor can kneel in prayer,
       And praise God's Name so true;
    And to the one who labored hard
       With words and works divine
    We honor him that manly priest,
       Our father, James O'Brien.

12   We'll entwine a wreath of evergreen
       And in the center place a name,
    Its our beloved Mrs. Morris K. Jessup,
       Whose noble deeds are known through Maine;
    Her charity was unbounding,
       Her heart was ever just and true,
    Her spirit's pierced that silent vale,
       And bade her loving friends adieu.

13   I wish I could remember all,
       And speak their names to you,
    But time and space will not allow
       What I would wish to do;
    And when the summer days have waned
       And to your homes returned again,
    May pleasant memories bring to you
       Of happy hours way down in Maine.

Mount Hope Chapel

Respectfully Dedicated to the Faces We Loved

By JOHN J. FRIEND, BANGOR, MAINE

1   I wandered to old Mount Hope's Gate
      And stood within the ground,
    And as I gazed along the path
      Where rose up many a mound,
    I thought of those we loved so well
      When life was young and bright,
    Whose bodies rest beneath the sod
      Now hidden from our sight.

2   Now General Varney, he lies here
      In life so just and true,
    And Franklin A. Wilson his beloved friend
      Whose name is known to you;
    And standing by that sacred spot
      That mark their narrow beds,
    The silent tears steal gently down
      Upon the honored dead.

3   Now Colonel Pullen is buried here
      In life was honored too,
    And Horace C. Chapman whose name brings back
      Sweet memories unto you;
    With Professor Ropes whose name was loved
      Have reached that far-off shore,
    His spirit's pierced that silent vale
      He's only gone before.

4   I'm standing on the hillside
        Where thousands they lie here,
    Whose pleasant smile and gentle voice
        Was to our hearts most dear;
    As in their narrow beds they lie,
        The thoughts they come and go,
    Of faces that we loved so well
        In years so long ago.

5   I stood beneath monument
        That rose up toward the sky,
    And read the names of those I knew
        Who wandered forth to die;
    To save for us a Union
        In this land we love so true,
    Who gave their lives on the battlefield,
        In that old coat of blue.

6   Now Thomas N. Egery is buried here,
        And Congressman Boutelle,
    With Edward R. Adams and William H. Whitemore
        In life was known so well;
    And George D. Harden and Edward Neally
        Their bodies 'neath the clay
    Their spirits passed those gates ajar
        To the Eternal Day.

7   I'm looking at the old fort
        The dry leaves rustling 'round
    And memories they come back to me
        I hear the bugle sound;

And see those youthful faces
   With hearts and courage strong,
Who went forth to save the Union
   In the days of sixty-one.

8   To the mothers of our city
     Whose bodies they lie here,
   Whose words brought hope and happiness
     To memory ever dear;
   Their spirits passed to that bright shore
     And there's sure to come a day
   When you'll meet them on that morning
     When the mists have rolled away.

9   Mayor Robinson's body it lies here
     With Charles L. Chalmers too,
   And Palmers whose long years were spent
     In pleasant hours with you;
   They've passed beyond to that bright shore
     And in this life no more be seen
   And to the friends they left behind,
     Will keep their memory ever green.

10   The loving mother, she lies here
     The gentle sister too,
   The manly brother's voice is still
     The father loved so true;
   They all rest here in old Mt. Hope,
     To earth their bodies given
   And though they rest beneath the sod
     I hope their souls in heaven.

11   The Hamlins they are buried here
     And Stricklands you all know,
The Herseys and the Crosbys
     Were honored years ago;
With Albert Paine and James Dunning,
     With Leonard March lies here
And Dr. Pond who spoke to them
     Of christian hope most dear.

12   In old Mount Hope's most sacred earth
     The old stock they lie here,
Their manly forms and noble deeds
     To memory ever dear;
They built our city here below
     This Bangor we love too,
And in this life they took a part
     In what was just and true.

In Memoriam

Of John R. Graham now I speak
     A tribute I'll pay thee,
You always stood for what was just
     To help our good city;
And though your body's far away
     In Quincy's churchyard there
We hope your soul dwells with your God,
     Is Bangor's earnest prayer.

Cathedral of Rheims

Dedicated to Those Three Words:

Peace on Earth

By JOHN J. FRIEND, of BANGOR, MAINE

1   It's midnight, and as by the hearth
      The fading embers glow,
And visions they come unto me,
      Of scenes that come and go.
Of Europe and her mighty war,
      In battle's fierce array.
Then sheathe the sword, bring forth the plow,
      For peace this autumn day.

2   The homes we loved have been destroyed,
      It's lonesome everywhere.
The one who was our main support,
      Has left us in despair,
For we have bade that last good-bye,
      And clasped that gentle hand.
His body's in an unknown grave,
      In a distant far off land.

3   And Belgium, that little land,
      You were noble, just and true,
You stood for home and sweethearts
      And friends so dear to you,

And when the war is over,
  And peace returns once more,
They'll tell of your great sacrifice,
  In songs, from shore to shore.

4 Oh, Rheims, the world it feels the loss
    Of that historic pile,
  Where kings and queens, within whose walls,
    Have worn a heavenly smile.
  And with bowed head, and knee bent low
    Before the altar there
  They thanked the Giver of all good,
    For peace in silent prayer.

5 There standing on the hilltop,
    And the valley far below,
  Watching the contending armies
    As they move to and fro,
  And banners proudly floating
    Amidst the cannon's roar,
  Oh, Thou Great God of Nations,
    Bring peace to them once more.